SOS PODCASTS

Rosamaria Mancini

Copyright © Rosamaria Mancini 2024
All rights reserved.

Print ISBN 978-1-7384231-6-3

The right of Rosamaria Mancini to be identified as the author of this work has been asserted by her in accordance with the Copyright Designs and Patents Act 1988

No part of this publication may be reproduced, stored in a retrieval system, or transmitted in any form or by any means without the prior permission in writing of the publisher. Nor be otherwise circulated in any form or binding or cover other than that in which it is published and without a similar condition being imposed on the subsequent purchaser.

This book is a work of non-fiction based on the experiences and recollections of the author. Some names and characteristics have been changed, some events have been compressed, and some dialogue has been recreated to protect the privacy of others. The author has stated to the publisher, that except in such minor respects, the contents of this book are true.

Published by
Llyfrau Cambria Books, Wales, United Kingdom.
*Cambria Books is an imprint of
Cambria Publishing Ltd.*
Discover our other books at: www.cambriabooks.co.uk

REVIEWS

Anyone who has felt out of place and mystified by the otherness of their surroundings will love this book. New York to Italy, Italy to Germany, this is a wonderful chronicle of cultural confusion, heartfelt and very funny. Then there's the children — the author spins from mothering to over-mothering to worrying about over-mothering. Her one escape route is through listening to podcasts, finding solace through the voices she chooses to hear. Like any good friend, the reader will be on her side — at least mostly, she does admit to doing some crazy things!
David Britton, Director of Creative Writing, Swansea University

Funny, sharp, and observant, this balances homesickness and cultural curiosity with a hilariously frank and honest charm. Well worth lending an ear to.
Alan Bilton, Senior Lecturer, Swansea University.

Self-deprecating and irreverent, Rosamaria Mancini, who pitches up unexpectedly in provincial Germany, charts the loneliness of young motherhood in a foreign land where she understands little of the language and has only fellow military wives from the nearby NATO base for friends. Some chapters are pure stand-up comedy, on why she hates German Christmas markets or her in-laws' preference for drafty rooms, others, such as that on the death of her father, are poignantly moving. Rosamaria approaches each new challenge with the straight-faced aplomb only a New Yorker abroad could possibly muster but explains how she finds inner strength when she retreats to the world of podcasts.
Julian Preece, Chair in German, Modern Languages, Swansea University.

DEDICATION

To my family, in particular my parents Nicola Mancini (1940-2017) and Silvia Gigante Mancini.

CONTENTS

This is me	1
My life in Italy (before podcasts)	9
Where the fox and the hare say goodnight to each other	18
Gebären	28
Christmas (and a baptism) in Germany	40
Trying to worry less, parent more	51
Skimming in my 40s	65
XOXO podcasts	74
Catholic fidem	78
That crappy feeling	90
List, listen, cross through. Archive.	101
Eating in	113
Not blinded by the light	125
Needed: verb form of LOL	133
Productively isolating	147
Now what?	160
Acknowledgements	171
List of podcasts	173

This is me

I'm a big pain. I'm overbearing. I'm a lot to deal with, I know, especially because I'm not great at relaxing, at taking it easy. I can't help but feel torn all the time. I can't stop thinking about my family in New York. I can't stop worrying about my life in Germany with my husband and two kids. I always have a headache. I self-diagnosed some terrible terminal illness but no, thank God; my doctor says my condition is stress induced.

I think anyone would be this way if they were in my situation. I mean my life has been made up of one massive change after another ever since my first move from New York to Italy when I was a single woman with a career in the media. After almost 10 years there I moved on to Germany as a working mom. I never imagined all of this. I'm the youngest of four children brought up in New York by conservative Italian immigrants from Puglia. I grew up in the last two decades of the last century in a tight-knit Roman Catholic family in Brooklyn and Long Island. That's right, on the edge of the Big Apple. I worked hard in school. I wasn't nerdy, really, I wasn't. But I did always want to sit in the front of the classroom. I pushed myself and graduated from college with honors. In work I was ambitious, probably annoyingly so for some people, never satisfied with a job below my expectations. I then surprised everyone when I left everything in New York, including my family, and went to Italy where my parents came from for a job — nobody ever moves to Italy for work! (For one reason, the country still has one of Europe's highest unemployment rates.[1]) Except me. I saw an opportunity I could not refuse. So, for years, I have been an outsider — not quite an Italian, not at all a German, cut off from family. Who could I talk to? More

---

1. Destatis Statistiches Bundesamt. "June 2022. EU Employment Rate at 6%." Report. Web.

1

importantly, after an upbringing among Brooklyn parents, uncles, aunts, and an entire vocally opinionated clan with no "off" button, who could I listen to? More on that later.

I met my husband, Marco, an electronics specialist in the Italian Air Force, in Rome. Pretty soon we got married and then I gave birth to my/our first child, a daughter, named after my mother. I had settled in relatively well in Italy and spoke the language nearly like a native because it was the language of family life back home, but I realized now that I wasn't exactly doing most things the Italian way, even though in New York I had felt so Italian. Living in *Italia* somehow toned down my Italianity. I went from an overly proud *Italo Americano* to a stars-and-stripes, blueberry pie, patriotic American. I even framed a window-sized American flag and hung it in the center of my living room. I longed for big red, white, and blue holidays, like Independence Day, Memorial Day, and Thanksgiving. I returned from visits to New York with my luggage filled with pounds of ground American coffee and boxes of pancake and waffle mix. Taking American coffee to Italy…imagine!

Things got more complicated when my husband was assigned to a four-year post at a NATO base in Germany. I thought, "Please God, is this really happening?" I had, after about 10 years, just about figured out how to navigate Italian bureaucracy and live happily; it was a synthetic type of happiness perhaps, but it was still happiness. If we were going anywhere, I wanted to go back to New York. I had no interest in Germany or its culture. I was scared of that angry, hard-sounding language. I thought of Germany as this weird, annoyingly precise, rule-following place (their rules, not mine, which are perfect) which still had a no speed-limit *Autobahnen* — rules to suit BMWs! Strange, I told you. I knew the move would change my life the most. My husband would still be a part of the Italian Air Force and work with some of his Italian colleagues. Bravo for him. My daughter was only three years old, and she would adjust easily. But what about me? In Italy, at least I could understand the radio I had playing. But Radio Deutschlandfunk? Now way, Uwe!

I prayed on it. I'm a practicing Catholic despite living in such a non-Catholic age. I even worked for several years at the Holy See, the Vatican. The job was in Communications, among many things I helped manage relations with the English-speaking press at the Vatican's pilgrimage office. After praying, I typed up a lengthy Germany pro-and-con list. I talked to my folks back home, who basically said, "Germany bad, but marriage good." What help was that? None of this eased my anxiety and I practically developed a stomach ulcer. I had major stomach pain all the time. But it was "husband good" so that was it. I was moving to Geilenkirchen, GK as it was called for short, which turned out to be a small town in the most western part of Germany. It was no New York, no Rome, actually not even armpit New Jersey. It was in the middle of fricking nowhere. Nowhere being the borderlands of Germany, the Netherlands, and Belgium. So not even Bonn or Berlin. Gradually it sank in that I had agreed to move to an anonymousville, where there were more cows and sheep than people. I consoled myself with the thought that this was only for four years, not forever. I could survive. I would be okay. The base did have an American contingent (yes, wave that flag), but I wasn't the one in the military. I was just a wife, who wasn't tuned in. And, as it turned out, a soon-to-be pregnant mamma or, as I would have to learn to say, *Mutter*.

Yes, after a year at GK my daughter was joined by a baby brother. Please understand I'm completely devoted to them. But the stress! I'm always worrying about what they could and should be doing. Control freak? Damn right. It seems everyone around me doesn't care whether their kids have washed their hands after playing in the dirt, or what they're wearing in the cold, rainy weather, or what they're eating for a healthy snack. Am I the only one who is preoccupied by all this stuff? Am I a bad mother? Oh, those sins of commission and omission. Mommy, sister, anyone ... tell me I'm okay. I need your voice in my ear.

How do I cope? Well, I have a lot of self-made rituals and rules that I follow (all mine, not the made-in-Germany kind!), and honestly, it's exhausting to keep up with them, even for me. For example, I overdress my kids, I know I do. I can't let them out of the house without safety layers: waterproofs, hats, gloves, or scarves. In Germany, the weather is windy, wet, and rarely not freezing, but in my husband's opinion, I dress the kids according to how cold *I* feel. And I'm always cold. (I know he doesn't go for my oversized fleece polka dot pajamas but that's another story.) What really stinks is when all my effort and hard work doesn't pay off. I learned during a surprise visit to school that my daughter immediately takes off a layer as soon as she walks into the building. I'm disappointed when I pick up my son from daycare and he's brought outside to me without his arctic gear on. I want to say something. I don't understand why they can't put his jacket on. But I hold back. I try not to complain about these kinds of things. After all, I want them to treat my son well. So I quietly and quickly get him into the car. No time for kisses and hugs — he doesn't have a warm coat on.

Ok, ok, I know, I'm overprotective and underconfident. Like I said before, I'm a big pain. But until I moved to Germany, I didn't realize that I'm also a lonely, isolated big pain. So, what happens is, I look inwards at myself and the kids. And what I want is perfection. Need, not want. It's a must-have. And since I can't have it, I need something, or someone, to tell me my imperfections are acceptable. Kooky, yes. Crazy, maybe. But fun? Please.

So where can I find an opinion which says it's understandable that I adore white, cotton undershirts? I make sure my kids wear one every day, all year long. As a kid, I always wore what my mother called the *maglietta della salute* (translation: health shirt) and I still do. In the winter they work well as an extra layer of warmth, and in the summer they are a great sweat barrier. I don't want my kids walking around in sweat-soaked shirts, that's gross. I also want to protect their skin from synthetic fabrics. When my husband dresses them he sometimes passes on the undershirts and then my daughter teases me and says "na, na nah na, I don't have an undershirt on." I am annoyed by that, it's not funny. And it's not my fault that my son was surprised to see what he called his "naked" knees when my husband put a pair of shorts on him. If it's always cold out, I can't put the kid in shorts, come on, now.

I flush out their tiny noses using a nasal spray made with Italian thermal water almost every morning. I know they hate the smell of sulfur, but they don't have a choice. I learned all about the benefits of thermal nasal rinsing from my daughter's pediatrician in Italy who told me they help to remove snot and boogers. I was impressed. I tried an adult version myself and it reduced my sinusitis, which I had chronically suffered from in the past. I'm now a daily nasal rinser.

Also, I don't allow my kids to drink cold water. Room temperature only, please. And any beverage with ice is an absolute no-no. Cold water could interfere with their digestive process and might even trigger a vasoconstriction that could cause decompensation, even organ failure. I visited a high school friend in New York, and she offered everyone ice water, which made my kids, who have basically never been in contact with ice, very excited. My son kept screaming to his sister: "look, ice, ice, ice." I swallowed hard as I watched them raise their plastic cups and drink the cold water but as soon as they went back to play (and no one was watching), I removed all the cubes from their cups. I'm kind of okay with ice cream, but I make them wait a few minutes before I let them start licking away.

Cold air is also a curse, whether it comes from mother nature or man-made. In Rome, almost every Italian I spoke with was obsessed with the horrifying danger of the *colpo d'aria*, basically a blast of cold air on your head, neck, or throat. I was repeatedly told to "watch out" because it could lead to a cold, rheumatism, heart failure, you name it. So I hate air conditioning now. It's pure evil, which shows how un-American I have become in at least one thing. In New York, everywhere is air-conditioned. If I go out, I don't sit just anywhere. I strategize. I scan the ceilings and walls of restaurants or even people's homes for HVAC grilles. I must look like some kind of building inspector. When I ask a waiter if the air conditioning can be lowered I almost always get "let me see what I can do," which basically means nope. To survive the ice age, I reach into my bag and pull out my indispensable summer scarf, you know one that's cotton, lightweight, not too hot but provides just enough warmth and protection. For my kids, I bring zip-up sweatshirts. Layers, always. I know all this is weird. I know. I know.

In Germany, I don't share these terrors of the cold and dirty world with others. (I am, though, coming clean with you as I put it all down here during my stay in *Deutschland*). Sure, I do get lots of attention, more like stares, when I'm hovering over the kids, but it's who I am. I'm good with me, really, that is what I tell myself. I don't want to change. I have my husband (who I think still loves me), and my kids. My family in New York who I'm very close to even though they live thousands of miles away. They get me; they understand what I'm all about. They do, honestly. Now that my father has passed my mother gets all my attention. I call her every single day, early in the morning, usually around 6:00 a.m. her time. That way I get a few uninterrupted minutes with her. I don't think she minds; she always tells me she's up. She's an early riser. Well, she is now.

I have an equally great relationship with my sister, who has always been intricately involved in my life. I share almost everything with her, including our many, many ailments. I know it's odd, but if I have pain in my neck, she understands because she says her neck is sore too. If she feels like she can't breathe, I'm with her because I feel that heaviness in my chest as well. Sometimes we even have menstrual synchrony. The theory is that when you spend time with another person who menstruates, your pheromones influence each other so that eventually, your monthly cycles line up (Where did I hear that? I'll explain later.) We share "that time of the month" and we don't even live near/close to each other, that's how in sync we are.

I will do anything for my family or anyone else that needs real help for that matter. I'm a reliable, supportive person. I go out of my way to assist, only it must be before 8:30 p.m. No night call on this emergency line, sorry. I can't help at night. I need to stick to my sleep schedule. So I put my kids to bed at the same time every day and that way we all can get enough rest. There's no such thing as staying up late in my home — whether there's no school the next day or it's the weekend. And if we go out, I make sure we leave early so that my kids can get to bed as close as possible to their normal time. And while everyone says, "come on, they'll sleep in" tomorrow. They don't, they wake up at the same time, sometimes earlier because their sleep was disturbed. I have woken them up from unscheduled daytime naps scandalizing my Italian mother-in-law who believes in unplanned snoozes. I try to convince Marco to go to bed early too, "it's something we can do together," I say happily, but he insists that he needs time to unwind. Me? I just want everyone in bed asleep. Where they should be. After 8:30 p.m.

Marco says that my bond with my New York family, especially my sister and mother, hasn't allowed me to form true friendships with other people. So now he's a psychologist? I thought I was just bad at making friends, especially since I have been trying to make them in my 30s and 40s, the so-called "sunken place of friendships."[2] I have made a few friends in more than a decade overseas, but only a very few, and these relationships have had their ups and downs. There have been outings with my husband's colleagues and their wives when I've felt him squeeze my knee tightly under the table. He wasn't being cute: he was trying to break my awkward silence, stop my continuous fake smiling, or get me to realize that I was constantly rubbing my nose, which oddly gets itchy when I'm feeling uncomfortable or out of place.

So that's me in Germany. A fish so far out of water that I might as well be in the Gobi Desert. To be fair GK does have about 27,000 inhabitants but they manage to stay politely invisible to me. I remain stressed, sleep-obsessed, and friendless. No family voices in my ear, not much radio I can relate to (or even understand). And then by accident of timing (this was 2017) I truly discovered a new savior (I told you I was religious). And his/her/its name was Podcast.

Oh, blessed Podcast! I thank God and all the angels and saints for David Winer and Adam Curry who created podcasts. Through them, I have access to people and content that have become my link to what's going on in the world, especially in the United States. They have helped me get ideas about the big issues I care about and find a perspective to help me form a view, on topics like femicides, wrongful convictions, student loan debt, anti-vaxxers, immigration, and climate change. And sure, some of it is basic and personal, but now I know how to make a dish with primary ingredients like celeriac and kohlrabi, which before Germany I did not even know existed. Podcasts have even helped me pray and meditate. And they've entertained me thanks to the few comedy and fiction shows I've accessed. I've laughed and gasped; I really have.

It's a chilly world both outside and inside for me. If it's not *colpo d'aria*, it's the damn itchy nose. So, I stick my earbuds in and listen.

---

2. Furlan, Julia, host. "Accept the awkwardness: How to make friends (and keep them)." *Life Kit*, NPR, 19 Aug. 2019. npr.org/2019/08/15/751479810/make-new-friends-and-keep-the-old?t=1660807568733

Podcasts help me to settle down. When I worked in journalism I was committed to gathering information, whether through newspapers, watching television, or listening to the radio. But podcasts have offered me easy, free, on-demand access to people and information — in the privacy of my own mind space. Podcasts have kept me almost sane and connected. They help me to unwind, to take the edge off. I don't think they are acting like a sedative impacting my central nervous system, but I do feel like they are a kind of listening therapy. My friends and family in the United States think I have this fascinating European life, but all I've been doing is trying to manage my isolation and better understand my identity and why I am the way I am. And podcasts have become my friends along the way.

The app on my smartphone is like my own giant library that I have easy and free access to. I go in, browse, download, and listen. I stick with the podcasts I enjoy and delete the ones that don't work for me. The fact that they are on demand makes it possible for me to stop during an episode and, say, collect my daughter from the bus stop or take my son to the bathroom when he needs to poop, and then start right where I left off the next free moment. I especially like this control factor because, as you have probably realized, my life is about order and rules. My order, my rules. But oddly with the help of my listening friends, they seem to be more aligned with the calm efficiency of Germany. Who would have guessed?

My life in Italy (before podcasts)

I loved Italy. I hated Italy. I felt both of those emotions strongly, all the time. I alternated back and forth, and it was often draining and stressful to live through the highs and lows but that's the kind of relationship I had with the *bel paese*.

I was charmed, smitten — all those lovey-dovey words — with Italy for all the obvious reasons. The old cities are beautiful, the small towns respect the past, and most of them are filled with art and architecture that anyone can easily and freely experience by looking and walking. In Rome, I couldn't get over the fact that my metro stop on the B line was 'Colosseo.' I would step off a graffiti-ridden train, walk up the stairs, and there was the Colosseum in all its glory for me to admire for a few seconds before I turned around and walked down Via dei Fori Imperiali, more eye candy for me. Sweet. Later I moved to Sermoneta, a small medieval town outside Rome and from my second-floor terrace, I could see the town's treasure — the 13th-century Caetani Castle. With its towers and drawbridge, it is all I imagined castles to be in my highly detailed childhood fantasy world. I also pictured myself living in one with my whole family — mom, dad, my two older brothers, and of course, my sister. I was delighted to see it each morning while I ate breakfast.

In Italy, my appetite grew exponentially, and it wasn't because I was developing diabetes or hyperthyroidism. I did worry about these, of course, and did get blood work done, just to make sure nothing was wrong with me. It turned out I was just excited and got caught up in all the new food choices. I shopped at different outdoor markets — imagine 10 different tomatoes and five different types of eggplants to choose from! I began to appreciate raw ingredients. I started to examine fruits and vegetables closely, looking at their color, size, shape, and firmness, like an Italian *nonna*. I didn't know exactly what

I was touching or feeling for, but it was interesting to gather this tactile information. I am not nerdy, I am not. But I started to appreciate different flavors and tastes. I began to enjoy wild boar ragu (yes, a sauce made with those rampaging wild animals that can destroy your car), deep-fried artichokes, chicory salad, fava bean puree, and buffalo milk mozzarella. I ate more, a lot more, and cleaned my plate, something I never did in New York where I always left a little something — even using bread to mop up any scraps that I couldn't get with my fork or spoon. Me, little Rosey — that's what my family calls me — cleaning my plate, acting somewhat gluttonous, shocker! Like a proper Italian, I started to finish each meal with a coffee, not a cappuccino, which I scandalously drank after meals when I first arrived. I didn't know it was a no-no to have a milk-based drink after a meal — it is, don't do it, at least not in front of Italians! I was happily intoxicated by the smell of coffee. I learned how to order and even got detail oriented with a *caffè macchiato al vetro*, coffee with a splash of milk in a glass cup, instead of porcelain or ceramic, because I enjoyed the higher and denser froth the glass cup offered. The glass also cleans better, and since I am all about hygiene, it became my preferred *tazza* of choice.

More importantly, though, Italy was dear to me because it's where my origins are, it's where my parents were born, raised, and married, and even where the remains of three of my *nonni* rest. My family is from Mola di Bari, a small town on the Adriatic Sea, just kilometers from Puglia's capital city of Bari. My parents migrated to the United States in 1969, just a few months after they were married. There were so many times when being in Italy made me feel good, it made me feel somewhat at home.

Yes, I grew up in New York, but it was an Italian-speaking home with *Pugliese* traditions. We celebrated most religious holidays with mass and traditional fare. For example, on St. Joseph's Day, 19 March, we eat *malfade* pasta with anchovies and toasted breadcrumbs. The long pasta with wavy sides honored St. Joseph's profession as a wood carpenter. And on Good Friday most of our extended family, including aunts, uncles, and cousins, squeezed into my grandmother's small Brooklyn apartment to eat *scalcione*, a calzone filled with salted codfish, scallions, anchovies, and Gaeta olives. The calzone, which took at least two days to prepare, marked the end of our Friday fasting during Lent. The leftovers were highly sought after, especially since this calzone was only made once a year.

My childhood home was a villa. The front yard was marked by a lawn shrine with a small grotto for the Virgin Mary, and in the back was the big garden with fruit trees and vegetables. My father planted a lot of everything, including *San Marzano* tomatoes, the oblong-shaped ones with the pointed end, and long, dark green string beans that we eat with spaghetti and tomato sauce, a traditional summer *Pugliese* dish. Then one weekend in August our deck was turned into a canning facility for tomato sauce. The work was hard — washing, cutting, boiling, straining, milling, and finally filling the mason jars. I especially liked running the electric mill, helping the plum tomatoes turn into red liquid gold. The result of the usual six bushels of tomatoes was about 70 jars of sauce, enough to get us through the winter months.

Growing up I didn't hear the stories of Snow White and the Seven Dwarfs or Cinderella, but instead my mother read and told me Italian fables like *Pinocchio* or *La Befana*. She also sang old folk songs like *Il grillo e la formica*[3] about a cricket and an ant who get happily married. And instead of feeding and getting her four children out of the way, she made us all wait until 8:00 p.m. for dinner, the usual time my father returned home from a long day of work at his auto collision repair shop. This wasn't about appeasing my father's ego; it was about spending time together. As I write this, I wonder at my own practice now — bed by 8:30 for everyone. Am I doing it wrong?

I found so much of my upbringing when I moved to Italy, the traditions, the love for family, the respect of others, and the communal table. I appreciated and admired it. It was the norm. I wasn't the odd one out anymore, which I sometimes felt when I would share things about food and family with my American friends at school — "ewwwwww, you eat that?" they would say.

As a journalist, I covered *L'Eroica*, a vintage bike race in Gaiole in

---

3. Raganella La Raganella. "Il Grillo e la Formica." *YouTube*, uploaded by Raganella La Raganella. 22 June 2010, youtube.com/watch?v=4C0w2lnS9hs

Chianti in Tuscany, where Italy's premier red wine Chianti is made. The race with about 5,000 participants re-enacts historical cycling with authentic bicycles and jerseys. The idea behind the race, held in October since 1997, was to preserve Tuscany's gravel roads from being covered by asphalt. I was enamored by this modern-day exaltation of history. I also had loads of fun that weekend learning about wine therapy, an extension of the wine tourism industry in Tuscany, that includes bathing, cleansing, and exfoliating with the stuff. Cool, right? To celebrate our first wedding anniversary, my husband and I spent the weekend at an *agriturismo* in *Manciano* near the Terme di Saturnia, also in Tuscany. Our stay in the farmhouse resort included dinner at a long, wooden table outside with all the other guests at the farmhouse. The meal was collective, all together at the same time, and it was surprisingly lovely. How could it be that uptight, guarded, nervous me could feel so relaxed in that company? The air? The wine? The sense of family?

When I was pregnant with my daughter, Italians put me on a super high pedestal. I never waited for anything. I was always told to go ahead in restaurants, supermarkets, everywhere. I had random people watching my diet, making suggestions about what to and what not to eat. Unlike my mother-in-law (more on her later) I didn't find them invasive but instead found they were thoughtful. The brothers at my local newsstand at the Latina train station were worried about me taking the train each day to work. They thought it wasn't right and that my employer, the Vatican, had done me wrong. I told them not to worry and assured them that it was *tutto bene*. I was doing well. You wouldn't expect from Italy's figures for new births, which totaled just 420,170, a 4.5 percent decrease from the previous year,[4] the lowest level since the unification of Italy in 1861, but women in Italy have a generous maternity leave package. They are guaranteed up to five months of leave at full pay and can take six months more at a reduced salary if they choose. Plus, they have two hours of early leave each day for breastfeeding until the baby is one year old. These types of benefits don't exist in the United States. The only people guaranteed

---

4. "Bilancio Demografico Nazionale." *Istituto Nazionale di Statistica*. 13 July 2020, istat.it/it/archivio/245466

paid leave are federal employees, who get six weeks. For most women it's more like: have a baby, use your vacation time to stay with your newborn for a few weeks, and then get back to work asap before some other person takes your job!

In Italy, families with children are always welcomed. Italians really love kids. Every time we ate out, the first thing the wait staff did was ask what they could prepare for the baby. There are no kids menus in Italy with processed chicken nuggets or fish sticks, they just make smaller portions of adult food like pasta or pizza. My daughter's order went to the kitchen immediately and then they returned with a bottle of room temperature, natural, spring water for her to drink — remember, too cold hurts a child's tummy! Lastly, the Italians were kind to me, even though I wasn't an Italian in the traditional sense — born and raised in the country. I'm fluent but my American accent can be heard after speaking just a few words. Then most people — colleagues, acquaintances, hairdressers, cashiers, doctors — asked where I was from — "New York," I would proudly say — and then they would get excited and want to practice their English with me. I often found their English difficult to understand, but I always appreciated the effort. I felt welcomed, never frowned upon. I also really liked being called *bella* (beautiful) and *tesoro* (treasure) all the time. I mean who wouldn't, it did wonders for my ego. I always felt so pretty, even on bad hair days.

But I also couldn't stand Italy, I really detested it, for just as many reasons. I found it impossible to escape the red tape that was everywhere, making simple things, like bank transactions or mail delivery, complicated and oftentimes impossible. I had one awful experience after another at Poste Italiane, the Italian post office, a former state-owned monopoly that became a public company in 1998. The post office is still completely controlled by the government — the Italian Ministry of Economy and Finance is its only shareholder. I was told when I arrived that it was "easier" to open an account at the post office, which also doubles as a bank. Not true. I opened a checking-type of account and left the branch with just paperwork, no temporary debit card. I waited over a month before the card arrived but still couldn't use it because then I had to wait for the pin to arrive separately in the mail. I asked the post office/bank what the next steps were if it didn't arrive. They said it was *complicato*, I would have to cancel the existing pin, wait for confirmation, and then they would reissue another one in the mail. I was agitated. I needed a bank card, now! I knew this would have been easily resolved in any bank branch in New York.

The postal system in Italy is world-famous for its delays, lost letters, and disgruntled employees. In 2006, an Italian woman was 10 years late for a medical checkup[5] because the letter notifying her of the appointment arrived 10 years after it was sent. In 2018, a former postman was found with 400 kg of undelivered mail — bank statements, bills, private correspondence — in his home.[6] The postman said he was fed up with his low salary and hadn't delivered mail for three years. He was one of a string of postal workers found with undelivered mail in their garages and cars. I felt like I was experiencing a part of the Austrian writer and poet Ingeborg Bachmann's novel *Malina* where she wrote of a mailman who ceased distributing mail and accumulated it in his three-room apartment piling up to the ceiling.

Then when I needed services in-house at the bank it became a test of my will and my patience. I questioned myself — Do I really need to do this? Is there an alternative, another way? I mostly used the big, beautiful branch at Piazza San Silvestro in Rome's city center, right near the Prime Minister's buildings and other Parliament offices. The Neorenaisssance style building was once a monastery. On one of my first visits, I selected what services I needed on the touch screen and out came my number. "How efficient," I thought. I was number 312. I looked up to see what number they were assisting, and I saw 230. I thought, "it's a mistake, yes, a mistake." I immediately went to the front desk and said smiling, "Excuse me, I think the system is broken because there are about 100 people before me?" I was firmly told that it was lunch and that I had to wait. What? This was unfricking

---

5. "Italy: 'Letter' late than never." *UPI*, 5 April 2006, www.upi.com/Odd_News/2006/04/05/Italy-Letter-late-than-never/69491144272459/

6. Giuffrida, Angela. "Former postman found with 400kg of undelivered mail in Italy." *The Guardian*, 6 April 2008, theguardian.com/world/2018/apr/06/former-postman-found-with-400kg-of-undelivered-mail-in-italy

believable.

I once even tried home delivery of a daily newspaper. I thought it would be great to get the paper at home every day. I have always been old school, even in my 20s and 30s, yes that's me. I could grab it and go, like I did in New York. I learned quickly that in Italy there aren't paper routes that young people hold as a part-time job, the post office, ughhhhhh, handles most mail delivery, including daily newspapers. I received Monday, Tuesday, and Wednesday papers on Thursday and then Friday, Saturday, and Sunday papers the following Tuesday or Wednesday. I complained to deaf ears. Why wasn't the mail delivered every day? They told me nothing could be done. I sadly canceled the subscription; my newspaper delivery dream was not happening in Italy.

The train system was also horrible, like a colonoscopy prep, the purgative part that includes taking a powerful bowel-clearing substance and coping with the resulting diarrhea. (Yes, I had one of these. I will get to that later too.) Except in Italy, I was experiencing it daily. When I moved to Sermoneta, I commuted to Rome. The train ride was listed as 35 minutes long. I considered myself an experienced commuter. In New York, I rode the Long Island Rail Road (LIRR) into Pennsylvania Station for several years. The LIRR is the busiest commuter railroad in North America, carrying an average 300,000 customers on over 700 trains each day.[7] In Italy, though, my skills were worthless because TrenItalia, the state-owned train company, is its own beast. I was up-in-arms daily about cancellations, delays, overcrowdedness, malfunctioning heat and air conditioning, leaky windows and roofs, and doors that didn't open. At least a few times a week I heard an announcement that my train was late because of a "delay in the train's preparation." What does that mean? Why didn't they prepare the train? I couldn't understand, but there was nothing to understand, that's just how things were. I was always upset, agitated, and pissed off. I wanted to yell. I wanted to vent with the Italians. I wanted them to nod their heads in agreement with me. I thought we could protest these injustices together, we could start a

---

7. "Long Island RailRoad General Information." *Metropolitan Transit Authority*, web.mta.info/lirr/about/GeneralInformation/

revolution of sorts, but I rarely found anyone who was as worked up as me.

For the most part, the Italians were calm, relaxed, and resigned to their fate on the train or at the post office. I wanted to believe they were more worried about the country's bigger problems, like the corrupt politicians in office, the mafia's stronghold on society, the archaic education system teaching kids Latin (who speaks Latin?) instead of good English or Mandarin, the high sales tax at 22 percent, and the failing public health care system. They were worried, but not enough to get agitated and raise their blood pressure like me. I recalled my father's words, who even though he missed and loved his homeland was often frustrated by the Italian ways and said, "Italians only think about soccer and food."

So, Italy. I privately enjoyed the positives, and complained a lot about the negatives, mostly to Marco. As you'll have noticed, I may be short of friends but I'm not short of opinions. Maybe that's my problem. Opinions. I often comment during radio or television newscasts, and Marco finds it irritating because he says he can't hear what's being said. I find that odd because I can still hear perfectly. I appreciated that Marco always said that he was "sorry" that I had to experience the worst of Italy, as well as the best, as if he was part of the problem because he was Italian but then he always said, "that's just the way things are." That was exactly what I didn't want to hear.

I could have used some advice, encouragement, a plan of action. I got nothing from him or anyone else. I just dealt with it alone. I didn't think I was going to be living in Italy forever. I was just there temporarily, until my husband retired. I did the simple math, over and over, he enlisted at 21 years old, which meant that he could retire at around 45 years old, and then we would move to the United States, the East Coast, obviously New York, where my family lived.

This was life before podcasts. Sure, I knew they existed, even had my j-students at the university I taught at study them as a "new" storytelling medium, we looked at the podcasts *Serial* and *StartUp*, but I didn't understand their potential, what they offered. I just didn't get it, yet. So with no helpful voices in my ear, I spent my private time dreaming of that next move, back to New York. Sure enough, the move came, but not across the Atlantic — it was across the Alps, to Germany.

Where the fox and the hare say goodnight to each other

The move to Germany was completely unexpected, a big surprise. I thought I knew what I was getting into when I married Marco in San Giovanni della Pigna, a beautiful, bonboniere-like church in Rome's historic center. Like I explained, Marco was in the military, but it was the Italian Air Force where deployments or assignments overseas are rare. In fact, they are highly sought after and difficult to get because of all the benefits. So, I never worried about moving and leaving everything behind every few years because Marco's permanent duty station was Rome. In more than 10 years, Marco had only one major deployment to Afghanistan, and obviously I didn't go with him. That wasn't until Marco dropped the job-in-Germany bomb and with that decision his career trumped, more like trampled over, mine.

I am still learning to accept that Marco's work is number one, it comes first. I have very little control, and imagine how difficult that is for me, in this part of our relationship. Am I resentful? No. But does it bother me? Yes, a bit. I have a lot of pride. I know it's uncatholic to have too much pride. I'm aware that humility is important and that I should be humble, but I don't always feel or act that way. I liked my career and was proud of it, but I temporarily put it on the side and that's somewhat painful. I feel bad sometimes. I try not to think about it too much and focus on where I am right now, which is GK.

From an operational, day-to-day perspective, GK and the surrounding area are practically flawless, especially when compared to Italy. The streets are perfectly paved and pothole free. In Italy, one of our two cars, an ancient silver Audi A4, sounded like a tank on tracks, but here it made less noise, the ride was smooth. I guess it was made to drive on these German roads; our Audi was back home. The spruce and pine trees are cut by maintenance crews before the rainy and windy seasons begin. In Italy, I never saw a tree being cut until someone was killed by a fallen branch or tree. In 2018, fallen trees killed three people near Rome and one in Naples after strong winds.[8] In Germany, street sweepers are a real thing. I'd never seen one in Italy. And they work on a set schedule. There is little to no trash on the side of the roads. It all seems perfect, especially because I don't watch local news or read the papers.

In Waurichen, the tiny village just outside the GK town center where we rented a 140-square-meter passive house (an energy-efficient home with a reduced carbon footprint), there are clean-looking cows going about their passive business. Chickens and ducks too. There are stables with perfectly groomed horses and ponies. It's like a children's toy farmyard. According to the latest census data,[9] 730 people live in a village that's about half a kilometer from one end to the other. Surely this is wrong. Did they add a zero? It feels more like 73 to me. I hardly see or hear anyone. If by some miraculous coincidence I do run into someone during weekdays, they are polite and say *hallo* or *morgen* but with a non-committal expression, as if their zygomaticus major hurts too much. Like in Silent Night (a German carol of course), 'all is calm, all is bright.' I know Italian and Americans. They are expressive and loud. I can sometimes hear my kids playing from outside, which for them often includes laughing and even screaming. I don't, though, hear our neighbors' children. I guess they play silently, 'calm and bright'. The weekends are scary, practically noiseless. I start to believe there is a 2:00 p.m. curfew because everything shuts down and the streets are deserted. The only sign of life I see on the weekends are the garbage bins that are already curbside late Sunday morning passively ready for their early Monday pick up.

---

8. "Three Killed, One Missing in Storms." *ANSA*. 29 Oct. 2018, ansa.it/english/news/general_news/2018/10/29/three-killed-one-missing-in-storms_f35ff77e-0d41-4dac-8164-63c033a871ea.html

9. Waurichen in Heinsberg (Nordrhein-Westfalen)." City Population. 8 Sept. 2015, citypopulation.de/en/germany/settlements/nordrheinwestfalen/heinsberg/05370012x076P__waurichen/

If and when the sun comes out (and that's not a normal thing in these parts) the locals go walking with trekking poles, an accoutrement that I honestly don't get. And the others pull out their expensive-looking bicycles and start riding on the trails that run through the surrounding farmland (the right kit is everything). I am not a big fan of these trails, if I'm walking I want to be going somewhere, not blundering around in what feels like a scary corn maze. Being in the middle of nowhere is bad enough. Getting lost in nowhere land is worse. So I started to spend more time indoors like the locals. And that's how my love affair with podcasts began. I use my phone. I use my smart speaker. I need easy-going, low-maintenance friends like Sarah May from the *Help Me Be Me* podcast. I want to hug her because she told me that everything I was feeling when I first arrived in GK — nervous, insecure, worried — was okay, was acceptable. And I really needed to hear that from someone other than my mother and my sister. I needed to hear from someone who doesn't know and love me. I also took bits and pieces of her advice. I learned in one episode that if I have feelings I don't like or want[10] that I need to face them, talk about them, not block them out. I picked up a recalibration exercise to help me deal with FOMO,[11] you know, fear of missing out. Because I did feel when I arrived in GK that I was missing out on the world, on information and events. I needed a connection and I needed it in my comfort language — American English. I began to listen to the *NPR* podcast *Life Kit*. The podcast's different hosts gave me tools to deal with big and small challenges. I felt like I was getting access to public information resources from back home: how to get the best from your doctor, how to pay off your student loans the right way and so on. I really liked it. I found it useful but more so I felt connected.

 I do have to get air, though. Yes, even me. So, I go for walks in the village — up the block, around, back, repeat — earbuds in,

---

10. May B., Sarah, host. "What to do When You Have Feelings you Don't Want to Feel." *Help Me Be Me*, Episode 87, 28 Nov. 2016. soundcloud.com/helpmebeme/ep-86-what-to-do-when-you-have-feelings-you-dont-want-to-feel

11. May B., Sarah, host. "Chronic FOMO: A Recalibration Exercise." *Help Me Be Me*, 3 Sept. 2016. soundcloud.com/helpmebeme/chronic-fomo-a-recalibration-exercise

listening to my podcasts. I peek into my neighbors' homes, especially those with nuclear fallout center signs. These homes have an enclosed space to protect people from radioactive debris or fallout from a nuclear explosion. And you thought I was paranoid. I also venture out of the GK area and go to our nearest city, Aachen, about 35 kilometers away. I don't pronounce Aachen correctly, (no one understands me when I say it) because like many native English speakers, I have trouble with the German hard CH (and the consonants in general) — it's all so in the throat. I was told that I didn't need my vocal cords for the hard CH. I had to press the back part of my tongue against the soft palate. I found this a bit too technical for my mouth. I knew of Aachen because I remember learning in school that it was practically razed to the ground during WWII. Memories are buried deep. Maybe that's why houses have nuclear shelters. The Battle of Aachen was a 19-day urban war, block-by-block, building-by-building, between the Americans and Germans. For the Americans, the city was of little military value, but psychologically important because its capture would be a break in Germany's main defensive line on the Western border. These days Aachen has appeal: There are people, a lot more people, shops, restaurants, and even universities — though none where I could work as an adjunct communications lecturer, like I had done in Italy. It also has a claim to be the birthplace of Europe because of the connection with Charlemagne, the first Holy Roman Emperor, who is buried in the cathedral.

If I need to get out of the village quickly, I go to the nearby GK NATO base — my husband's workplace. The Geilenkirchen NATO Air Base is a big deal. It's NATO's early warning hub, designed to pick up signs of possible attack from the East. It has 3,000 military personnel, drawn from 16 different NATO countries. When I visit I can see these weird Boeing E-3A Sentry planes taking off and landing. They look like the friendly passenger planes I took when I vacationed overseas to Italy as a child — except that they have a sinister-looking pancake thing on the top. Some kind of radar. Basically, GK is the eyes and ears of the Western Alliance. Two thoughts: 1. Eyes and ears. That's me and my podcast walks. 2. Maybe the home nuclear shelters are not so crazy. For us military wives (I hate that term) the

GK NATO base has shops and places to eat. There are wives from all over the Western world. Lots of Americans and about 40 Italian spouses. I never had much to do with military wives in Italy because I always had my own job, even after becoming a mother and changing to a baby-friendlier occupation.

At GK I realized quickly that the Italian wives are like a preppy, loud cheerleading squad. I didn't really like cheerleaders in high school; I found them annoying with their color-coordinated outfits and pom poms. I think all non-cheerleaders feel that way, maybe we're jealous. Maybe we're sulky. I don't know. The military wives know everything about GK. They know about the shops and which ones accept our tax-exempt status, they know the calendar of the local Oktoberfests, and they know who the best doctors and dentists are in the area. They truly are a wealth of information. They like spending time together. I was asked early on by a few Italian wives to go shopping, but not for clothes or shoes, which might have been okay, even though GK is the opposite of fashionable. But for food, more specifically to the German discount chain stores to pick up the special sale items of the week. I wanted to die. I couldn't do this…group food shopping, please no! Where the hell am I? Is this what my life has become? I lied, multiple times. I said I had to pick up my daughter early from school. I said I had a dentist appointment. I said I had to work on my PhD, which I started when I moved to GK. I wanted a project, something big, to keep me busy and help me feel as if I was working towards something, especially a future career. I couldn't just cross through the days of the calendar until it was time to leave. I used any excuse rather than join a shopping-cart rodeo.

I do see the wives on base, especially if I eat lunch with my husband at the dining facility. I say *ciao ciao* and try to quickly move away or I put my head down. I know, I should be embarrassed, that's really childlike. I can't always escape them. I know that God is trying to teach me something: "My child let down those barriers!" But I can't. I remember the day one wife walked over to my table while I was having lunch with my husband and asked if she could join us. I wanted to say "no," but instead I said "sure." She scooted me over and started chit chatting about random things — the weather, the schools … Then when she noticed the sliced bread next to the pork schnitzel on my lunch tray the conversation turned to how much her husband and kids adore the homemade bread she makes with sourdough starter a few times a week. "Do you want a piece of my starter? I can give it to you!" I was puzzled. I have what's called a 'resting bitch face;' people think I'm irritated or annoyed when I am relaxed or thinking. I'm not, really. Plus, I am also an externalizer, one of those people who show their emotions on their face. Great, right? And so she started talking all about the starter, explaining that it would need care and that it must be kept in a large glass jar in the refrigerator and fed equal parts water and flour every few days. If it's not fed, she said dramatically, "it will die and grow mold!" I nodded and said *"wow, interessante"* but what I was really thinking was why doesn't she just buy those little packages of yeast from the store ... they work fine, right? Plus, how much bread, could she possibly be making. I never made bread before. I must be an awful wife/mother to my Italian husband and children. I have made Focaccia every so often. But this is Germany, and there are so many different types of *Brot* and *Brötchen* here. I would say bread is one of the few, I said few, culinary things that the Germans do pretty well. Plus, honestly, I didn't need anything else to take care of; my kids were plenty enough. I didn't suggest a time for the yeast to be handed over. I never brought it up again. I waved from a distance when I saw her again. But I'm sure the starter dough moment was when she started to hate me.

I know all about the wives and their happenings thanks to their WhatsApp groups. I was told firmly by one of the group administrators that the "Italian Club" group chat is only for official GK base communications and therefore I shouldn't share anything light or frivolous. Okay. So there's another group chat called "Little bit of everything," a free-for-all. The messages range from what's the best product to remove oven grease to who offers cheap pressotherapy (disgusting, lymphatic drainage!) to where to buy Italian brands of frozen vegetables. The "everything" group chat wives are obsessed with morning greetings and send them in the form of GIFs, memes, images, and videos. They are all over the Saint Days and write something like "Happy St. Day to all the Lucia's out there." And almost everyone in the group responds with either a thumbs-up emoji (I am not a big fan of emojis), congratulations, or a thank you.

The wives go deeper on Italian national holidays, such Liberation Day (25 April), Republic Day (2 June), and Armed Forces Day (4 November) with long messages, often citing words from the Italian Constitution. Okay I know I rave about Independence Day and Thanksgiving, but this is my story, my rules! The wives also share lots of pictures of themselves at various breakfasts or at on-base gatherings. They are great, self-documentarians. I am bombarded with these types of messages all day long. The pics and videos were eating up my smartphone's memory. I started getting push notifications that my 50GB of storage is almost full thanks to 49.4 GB of photos and videos. What to do? I considered leaving the group, I didn't want to look like a snob. Too late. That ship already sailed.

The wives gossip like high schoolers, which partly explains why they refer to each other as *ragazze*, girls, even though most of them are older than me and in their 40s and 50s. I learned exactly how they felt about me one night when we went out for dinner with my husband's colleague, Matteo, his wife, Marina, and their son Luca. I didn't organize the evening out, my husband did. I talked to Marina (scratching my nose every once in a while) and the topic of discussion was the wives. Marina clarified that she doesn't gossip (yeah, sure…) but the wives do, and they talk about everyone. I then made the obvious mistake and asked, "So, what do they say about me?" And she said bluntly, "They think you're an introvert and don't like to talk to people. They also think you're not fond of children." I laughed; I didn't know what else to do. My noes to shopping, my no to yeast, my silence in group chats. They had all been noted. But I felt bad. I thought I was going to cry but I pulled myself together. Let's be clear, I do like kids, I do, really, but I don't go crazy about them. I don't "oh and ahh" over other people's kids. I never have, it's not my way. I think it's weird when people are really interested in kids — why are they interested? what do they want from them? — and so I keep my distance from their kids as I would like others to do from mine. The word introvert, well, I have heard that before. If I argue with my husband, he often throws in the "anti-social" word. Not true, not true. I do like people. Just not all of them and just not always. I want to choose.

My podcast host buddy, Julia Furlan (note: I have never met or seen her before) knows exactly what I am talking about. She gets that it's uncomfortable to make friends and in fact in an episode of *Life Kit*[12] she said that opening yourself to new people sounds worse than getting a mouth full of root canals." Like I said, some of these podcasters really understand me. If I had to choose dental work or a cocktail party where I don't know anyone, the choice is obvious — opening wide and saying awwww!

In the *Life Kit* episode Heather Havrilesky, an advice columnist for *New York* magazine, said that the 30s, my age group when I arrived in GK, are the worst for friendships. Havrilesky said most people assume that everyone already has friends, but that's wrong because most people are still trying to make new friends. She said confidence is everything; that people will "like you more than you think they will." All good advice. The thing is that I don't think I have a confidence problem, I don't have trouble voicing my opinions or ideas. I probably should shut up a bit more. I have, though, always hated the awkwardness of talking to new people when there isn't an agenda or goal. I'm not alone in this.

In my work in the media and teaching I was one of many who would talk easily in a work environment but couldn't do social chat. Different skills, I guess. That's why I'm not great at small talk. I also felt the Italian wives didn't consider me Italian at all. To them, I was a *straniera,* an American, even though I grew up Italian, or at least I thought I did, and I learned Italian as a child. My paternal grandmother, who lived most of her life in the ground floor apartment of our three-family home in Brooklyn, refused to learn English. The only words/phrases she knew were "how much?" and "thank you very much," which she used when she went shopping. My *nonna* was quite refined, silver hair always in place, and she smelled citrusy thanks to the Jean Nate after bath splash she religiously used. She only wore dark blue and black clothes (she mourned my grandfather's death for 40 years) on her thin frame. I never saw her in pants, she didn't own any. I helped her to cook and bake; she would

---

12. Furlan, Julia. "Accept the awkwardness: How to make friends (and keep them)." *Life Kit.* NPR, 19 Aug. 2019. npr.org/2019/08/15/751479810/make-new-friends-and-keep-the-old?t=16608112130 17

give me a dollar or two if I turned the crank on the pasta machine at least 100 times. I especially liked being able to talk to her without everyone understanding what we were saying. I was proud of our shared language. I think I have inherited a similar genetic makeup because I look like her, at least sometimes. But this was not enough for the modern Italian NATO wives.

In New York I was happy with the brown bag lunches my mother prepared for me. In the school cafeteria, I pulled out *frittata* (before it was chic) and saucy meatball sandwiches on Italian bread, and all my friends annoyingly asked, "What are you eating?" I wasn't envious of their ham and cheese and peanut butter and grape jelly sandwiches (schools were not nut free then). I was annoyed that my teachers had turned my beautiful name Rosamaria into Rosemary. I was named after my maternal grandmother in Italy who only made one trip to America to be there at my birth. To please my teachers, I wrote and signed Rosemary Mancini; I applied to colleges with the name Rosemary Mancini. I had unwillingly accepted the name of an herb, one that I couldn't stand the smell or taste of. One of the first things I did when I got to college was fill out a change of name form at the registrar's office. So in name at least, I have chosen to be Italian.

I wish I did have more things in common with the Italian wives; the whole GK experience would have been easier. I would have had an easier time filling out the emergency contact information on school forms for my kids — that's always so hard. I would also have made some friends who were living a similar German experience. What do I say when they talk about the meals they make in their Bimbys, the expensive German-made kitchen robot they glorify in their homes like I do the Virgin Mary? Kitchen cult they maybe, but I don't have one. How do I not show my anguish when they ask if I want to wear traditional Italian dress and dance the *tarantella* at the International Wives Club? Smile and run away. How do I react when they start passionately arguing about who is the funniest comedian on an Italian sketch television show? I don't know, I don't watch that show. I do wish I could lose track of time when we are talking. I wish I could learn to giggle a little bit more. I wish I could take off my worry hat and feel carefree for a bit. But no, this type of socializing stresses me and makes me feel even more isolated, more out of place. I find that it's just easier to listen to my podcast host friends because they make me feel genuinely connected to others and also better about me and my life in nowhere land.

Gebären

Gebären: to give birth to; Kind auch to bear (old, form), to be delivered of (old); (fig liter: = erzeugen) to breed (Collins German-English Dictionary)

I got pregnant after only about eight months in GK, and no, it wasn't an accident. I guess I thought I could do it all during my German sabbatical, not just my PhD, which would help me with my future career, but a new baby too. I also really, really had to do it now. I was already in my late 30s and so if I was going to have a second child, it was now or never. I didn't know how much longer my body or I, could handle pregnancy. I also figured the new baby would be about school age when it was time to leave and then I could go back to work full-time. I really wanted to have a career again. I'm ambitious, is that so bad?

Just as importantly, I didn't want my daughter to be an only child. I wanted her to have someone blood-related, a sibling, that she could turn to when my husband and I were no longer around. I know, I know, it sounds morbid, but that's how I felt. I couldn't imagine life without my siblings, especially my sister. I was traumatized by my first birth in Italy and that's why it took me four years to even think about doing it all over again. By now I had managed to store the pre and postpartum away, far, far away in the back of my mind, especially because it included a lot of Italian style-drama, which meant it was gripping, intense, and highly emotional, especially because my Italian, non-English speaking mother-in-law, was one of the protagonists. She's Neapolitan and you know, they love the theater. Think Puccini or Verdi? Think Eduardo De Filippo and Antonio De Curtis, also known as Totò.

The start of my first pregnancy was calm and uneventful. I was dealing with my mother-in-law and her unsolicited advice. I felt she wanted to take over my small-framed body and tell it what to do, what exactly to eat, and what to wear. I don't want to stop working; it's good for me. I like peanut butter; it won't hurt the baby. I don't like ballet flats; they make my ankles look big. I listened to her. I respected her because she was my husband's mother, but her know-it-all ways overwhelmed me. But when my Obstetrician/Gynecologist (OB/GYN) was concerned about a possible birth defect after a routine ultrasound I forgot about my mother-in-law's meddling ways. I had an emergency amniocentesis and while it turned out to be nothing, I still had great anxiety up until the actual birth. I was also leaking urine between trips to the bathroom. I was leaking a bit more when I was sneezing and coughing. I was concerned, but I talked to my OB/GYN, and she told me that pregnancy caused changes in the bladder and the urethra. I wasn't doing Kegel exercises to help strengthen the muscle down there. I didn't know exactly what to squeeze and how long I should be holding the squeeze. But in the last weeks of my pregnancy, the leaks seemed more like giant flushes. I went for a routine checkup during Week 37 and they found that I was low on amniotic fluid. They scheduled a C-section. I was relieved that my parents had arrived in Rome by this point, I especially wanted my mother. Who doesn't want their mommy when they are going to deliver a baby? I did.

I wasn't disappointed or upset that I wouldn't have a natural birth because I didn't have a set birth plan. I had friends in New York (yes I still do have a few friends there), who were all about drug-free approaches to childbirth — no analgesics or anesthetics. No way. I was open to anything that made the whole experience easier, and that meant drugs of all kinds and types. I wanted the least amount of pain possible, that's it. I learned all the breathing techniques in a bi-weekly, two-hour how-to-give-birth class during my last trimester but if there was no need for the techniques then that was fine. I just wanted the baby, and me too, to be okay. I was the only *straniera* in the class and of course, everyone wanted to practice their English with me. I found it useful to compare bumps with the other women and learn how/what they were feeling at this point in their pregnancies.

I gave birth to a healthy, baby girl, at a private clinic in Rome's affluent Parioli neighborhood. This was possible thanks to the health insurance that the Vatican offered me as an employee at the time. They even gave me a bonus of about one month's salary after the birth, that's how serious they are about procreation! The clinic was quite a place, I read that former AS Roma player Francesco Totti's now ex-wife Ilary Blasi gave birth there. From the outside, it looked more like a hotel than a medical facility with its grand courtyard. The special, white glove treatment they offered included a bottle of Guido Berlucchi spumante brought to my private room. So my daughter arrived in style.

The C-section went smoothly, but the post-op was plain awful. I couldn't move. I was in terrible pain. The nurses put a wrap-around girdle on me (that I was told to purchase and put in my hospital bag!) and got me on my feet just 14 hours later. I walked up and down the hallway of the clinic like a 90-year-old grandmother slowly dragging my legs and what no longer looked like my cute size six, or 36, feet. I didn't recognize my ankles anymore, my lower extremities resembled loaves of white bread. I felt and looked awful – childbirth had destroyed me! I felt worse when I ran into the two other new moms in the hallway who had given birth at around the same time as me. They were squatting and bending, picking up their babies, they seemed so nimble. I hated them. I wanted to go home, even if I felt like crap. I was told that in order to be released I had to pass post-surgical poop, they needed to make sure my gut had returned to its pre-surgery state. I didn't know how this was going to happen. I could hardly move, how the hell could I squat on a toilet?

Meanwhile, my mother-in-law kept saying that she had been up and moving in no time when she had her boys; that "was one of the benefits of having a natural birth." I also tried to breastfeed my daughter in the clinic, but it wasn't working. I was in pain and there was blood coming out of my cracked nipples. My mother-in-law put her two cents in again. She insisted that I keep trying. She told me again that she breastfed her three babies and that it was "unnatural" to feed your baby formula. I couldn't take it anymore. I wanted to pull her soft platinum, blond hair. I know, a bit crazy, but my hormones were out of control. Please try to understand, I was overwhelmed. I couldn't really talk to my mother because my mother-in-law was always around and listening, even though she pretended to be doing something else while we were talking. I swear she had started to understand English. When everyone had left for the night and I was upset and crying, I called my sister in New York. She told me to "do what I had to do," and if that meant feeding my baby formula then it was okay. I told the clinic staff to bring me the stuff.

I also was overwhelmed by my little daughter. I didn't know how to hold and comfort her just yet. To be honest, I was a little afraid, especially after the nurses nicknamed her "the hawk" because she cried, more like screamed a lot. They stuck a binky in her mouth after just two hours. She held onto it, satisfying her sucking reflex. I could tell she was strong, so strong. God, help me, please! I stayed in the clinic for five days before I was released. I told them I pooped, but I had only passed a lot of gas. The situation at home wasn't any easier at first. I was still in pain and had trouble getting up and down from a chair, nonetheless my bed suddenly felt like it was a tatami mat. I also couldn't see well anymore, everything looked blurry in the distance. The pregnancy, the birth, caused my astigmatism and nearsightedness to return. I needed glasses and contact lenses again, ugh. I was part of the rare group of people (lucky me!) whose eyes returned to the level of vision they had before laser eye surgery. I was happy my parents had decided to stay for two months because I needed help and moral support. They were with me all day when my husband went to work. My mother changed the bandage on my wound and washed my hair in the shower.

So much for baby number one. Now, I was preparing for number two. This time in Germany I was still nervous about it all, but I felt a little more qualified because I had experience — been there, done that! And also had information from podcasts. I had help, support on-demand in a form that I could connect with easily. This was just so much better than searching for information on the web. Now, I didn't go on an all-out pregnancy podcast listening binge (that would make me more nervous than I already was) but I found a few podcasts that gave me information about things I had never thought about, as well as issues I was dealing with first-hand. I also liked hearing lots of different birth stories because they helped me to remember that every birth experience is unique. I was really into *The Birth Hour* podcast. The episodes are made up of first-person birth stories, vaginal, assisted, water, you name it, and this podcast has real moms talking about their experiences. I also spent time listening to the *Pregnancy Podcast*, which answered questions from listeners, usually expectant moms. I especially liked that the answers were based on facts and research. I felt more at ease about certain things thanks to host Vanessa Merten. I also enjoyed *Pregnancy Confidential*, a series of 32 podcasts designed to be accessed week-by-week. I liked it because it was informative but also light and funny with the hosts chatting it up like a group of girlfriends who curse once in a while. I missed that kind of talk in Germany.

I had already visited a local OB/GYN, or *Frauenarzt*, which literally means women's doctor, in GK for an annual check-up. I was happy that the doctor and staff spoke English and decided to have them oversee my pregnancy. I was given a small book called a *Mutterpass*, which means mother passport, that tracked all my updates and visits and was told to keep it with me at all times. I didn't have to go to a laboratory when it was time for routine blood work or glucose screening during my pregnancy because everything was taken care of in the office. In Italy I was running to the lab for everything. I went to doctor appointments with a large, manila folder filled with test results. And this time I didn't have an amniocentesis because there was now a non-invasive prenatal blood test, and all my markers were good. Aside from the morning sickness that thank God subsided after three months, I felt pretty good and made it through the first trimester without any hiccups.

In an episode of *Pregnancy Confidential* they talked about how important it was to put together a before-baby bucket list, that is you make sure that you do all the things you suspect you won't be able to do once the baby is there.[13] The hosts, which each week included a different group of editors from *Parents*, *Fit Pregnancy*, and *Baby*

---

13. Points, Dana, Debrovner, Diana, and Gail O'Connor, hosts. "Pregnancy Week 24 - Your Before-Baby Bucket List." *Pregnancy Confidential*. Parents. Dotdash Meredith. Season 1, Episode 16. 24 Feb. 2016. parents.com/pregnancy-confidential/pregnancy-confidential-podcast-week-24-before-baby-bucket-list/

magazines, explained that life as I knew it would be basically over once my second baby arrived (scary) and therefore the bucket list would be a good way to bond with my existing family before things changed. I didn't do this before my daughter arrived; even if I had heard of the idea, I was too concerned about her health to pay attention to anything else.

This time, though, I tried to go out to eat more (even though the food here wasn't to my taste), knowing that peaceful meals with two kids would be rare. Together with Marco, I organized two babymoons during my second trimester — a long weekend in Amsterdam (My mother-in-law came with us, and surprisingly she behaved quite well) and a 10-day vacation to Crete. I had fun in the Dutch capital visiting the Van Gogh Museum and cruising past canal houses and bridges. I walked a lot, what felt like kilometers, maybe even too much, but it felt good to be active and explore. I was excited to go to Greece. I wanted to eat fresh fish, and soak up the heat and sun, which I had longed for since moving to Germany. I already knew how to protect my fair skin from sunburn. (A fair-skinned Italian, where is the justice in that?) I didn't want to do anything that could hurt the baby or make me more uncomfortable than I already was. I packed a mineral-based sunscreen, no chemicals, and aloe vera. I also bought a wide-brimmed rattan straw sun hat and alternated time in the sun with time in the shade. I did, though, before flying start feeling some sinus pressure and pain, but since I suffer from chronic sinusitis I wasn't alarmed. I hoped the salty sea air would help me clean out my nasal passages and relieve my sinus pressure. It worked. My sinuses cleared — somewhat dramatically — while I was sitting on some of the loveliest beaches, including Elafonisi with its pastel pink sand and Balos with its vivid turquoise waters. I was better, in just a few days. The babymoons were successful!

When I returned, the women at GK Base Chapel where I attended Sunday mass regularly, started asking me questions about how I was doing and about my birth plan. The Chapel has a friendly Catholic community, mostly Americans with a few Italians as well. The families are enthusiastic about their faith. They also seem to like kids probably because they have a lot of them, somewhere between four and seven. (I counted them several times to make sure I got the number right.) I definitely didn't have enough kids compared to them. One wife asked if I was going to have a VBAC. "I had three of them," she said. "A what?," I thought. I had no idea what VBAC stood for. I hadn't heard about it in my podcast listening, at least not yet. I tried to act knowledgeable, but I had no clue. I responded, "I'm not sure." Then another spouse who had two boys talked about the "certain feeling, certain connection" moms have when they give birth naturally. She said, "When you start to feel their head, it's just amazing. You have to try to do it." I found her comment to be gross. I also thought it was outrageous and judgmental for her to think that she was more connected to her children because she had a natural birth. My daughter was super attached to me despite not coming out of my vagina.

I remember when my daughter was going to start daycare and at the orientation they suggested I pack a toy or stuffed animal that comforted her when she slept. The problem was that she didn't have one that she could bring along. The thing that comforted her was my hand through the bars of her crib. In the car ride home after mass I learned from a quick online search that VBAC meant 'vaginal birth after cesarean.' I later found a short episode of the *Pregnancy Podcast* about VBACs[14] and according to Vanessa Merten's experts I could have a VBAC in spite of already having one C-section because I didn't have a uterine rupture or a classical incision, that is a vertical cut in the upper part of my uterus. I had a horizontal cut and it was low, very low. I also listened to many first-person accounts of successful and a few non-successful VBACs in *The Birth Hour* podcast hosted by Bryn Huntpalmer.

But even though my first C-section recovery was challenging, I didn't want to try for a VBAC, now that I knew what it was. I had a C-section the first time around and I would have a second one, a final one. That's it. I entered my third trimester and told my *Frauenarzt* what my birth plan was — I had one, this time, woo hoo! — but he said that he wasn't going to deliver the baby and I needed to tell

---

14. Merten, Vanessa, host. "VBAC." *Pregnancy Podcast*, 6 July 2016, pregnancypodcast.com/vbac/?quad_cc

someone else. I didn't get it. I didn't understand. Is he going away on vacation near the end of my pregnancy? Oh no, he's retiring. He did look pretty old with scraggly white hair and thick glasses. Instead, he explained that in Germany, the *Frauenarzt* who oversees your pregnancy month-by-month is not there for the delivery. I would give birth in a hospital with the medical staff who were on duty at the time. I was surprised, disappointed, scared … I wanted him to be there, he at least understood me. I could, he explained, choose any facility I wanted because I wasn't tied to him. But I wanted to be tied to him, attached to him. I wanted him!

The big university hospital nearby is in Aachen, and I thought that it might work for the delivery. I went on the "pregnancy tour" with Marco and my daughter but the whole thing was in German and after 30 minutes of pure confusion we sneaked out. I didn't, though, have a comfortable feeling about the hospital, which felt so big, so clinical. I wanted something smaller, cozier, and that's why I also passed on the hospital in Mönchengladbach, near Düsseldorf, with its big, renowned maternity ward. The name, Mönchengladbach, was also a bit hard to pronounce, which contributed to my negative reaction. I wanted to be able to easily say the name of the city my son was born in.

I finally decided on a small, Catholic hospital in Stolberg, easy enough to pronounce and also close to home, just about 25 kilometers from GK. I knew it was the right place when I walked into the building and saw icons of Jesus Christ and the Virgin Mary. There they were, and I thought, "I'll be okay here." I went on a pre-visit, and they started showing me all the accouterments they had to help me deliver, such as gymnastic balls, wall bars, and hanging slides (to hold onto during labor…scary!), and birthing pools, but I didn't care about these things. I wanted to schedule my C-section. I asked if I could have it during Week 38, which would be perfect because it would fit right in with my mom's arrival and my daughter would not be on Fall break from school. The female doctor who already had a bit of a frown face started to look really upset. I could see that her jaw tightened up and she scratched slowly behind her ear. She told me that I should wait until my pregnancy came to term and have the famous VBAC. Not this again, errrrr. I told her no and that I just wanted a C-section. I had the right to choose, didn't I? She reluctantly scheduled it, and guess when ... the beginning of Week 40. I knew she was hoping I would give birth naturally before then. I was upset. I started imagining her with a broom and pointed hat. I left more scared than ever.

I wanted to share this experience on *The Birth Hour* podcast that I listened to regularly. I liked that the podcast was like a "safe place" where there was no criticism or judgment, just stories from moms willing to share some of the most intimate moments of their lives. I found the episodes, and there are many of them because the podcast has been around since 2015, to be like a type of personal monologue with just a few questions from the host. I wanted other women who chose or had to have a C-section not to feel as if it was wrong and unnatural. I didn't want them to feel stigmatized. Later during a routine checkup, my doctor found that the baby was putting pressure on my right kidney and that it was best not to wait. I had to have a C-section after all. Thank you, God! It was rescheduled for Week 38, in particular, 20 October, which was Marco's birthday. I asked if they could move it up a day or two, but they said, *nein, nein, nein*. I felt somewhat bad for my husband but there was nothing I could do.

I was thankful my mom had arrived just days before my scheduled C-section. She arrived with lots of gear — pajamas, onesies, burp cloths, bibs, and beautiful, handmade crochet blankets I would cover him up in. I knew it was a boy from the ultrasound during Week 20. I only had to pack his coming home outfit because unlike in Italy the hospital in Stolberg provided me with a fully stocked changing table that had everything needed to dress and take care of the baby. I was given a 5:30 a.m. arrival time and at 8:37 a.m. the baby, who we named after my deceased father-in-law, made his debut. I followed the *Pugliese* tradition of naming my children after their grandparents, just like my parents did. The idea was foreign to my made-in-Italy husband ... do you believe that! I had two drops in blood pressure during the C-Section, which didn't make me feel good and scared the crap out of me, and it also took longer than the doctors expected to close me back up. I understood the team of doctors when they told me what was happening. I was too weak and couldn't hold my son right away but he was doing well. I stayed in the recovery room a while and when I was brought back to my room, I found my husband bare chested with my son lying on him. I thought, "he's totally lost it!" I asked him, "what are you doing?" He said, "They told me to do it." I remembered learning about skin-to-skin contact, also known as Kangaroo Care, from my podcast listening and knew that it was one of the best things you can do to help your newborn to adjust to life outside the womb. I knew that it helped calm and soothe babies, improved their sleep, and even enhanced their immune system, but I thought it was for mom and baby. I didn't remember the part about dad and baby, but I found out later that I was wrong. I must have missed that but honestly I still found it a little bit weird.

I'm not sure if it was seeing my husband with the baby on his bare chest but I bounced back quickly this time around. I didn't get swollen legs or ankles. The white compression hosiery they put on me before the C-section helped. I actually liked the hose. I found them to be fun and cool, even somewhat sexy. I kept them on for about a week post pregnancy. I exaggerated; I know. I was also in less pain this time. I got up with just a little help from my mom and was moving around more easily. I didn't have to ask for painkillers all the time, which was great because while the doctors spoke English most of the nurses and other staff didn't understand me. I asked and a lot of them said they were from Turkey — Germany has the largest Turkish diaspora of any country in the world. Before arriving at the hospital, I did write down a few key words and phrases, including *Ich möchte etwas gegen die Schmerzen haben*, which meant "I want something for the pain." But I didn't think about the cut they made across my bikini line again because I also had my daughter to worry about. I didn't know how she would react to my son, especially because I hadn't received much feedback from her. I don't think she really understood what was happening, even though Marco and I tried to explain it to her, and so coming home with a baby who was going to live with us would be new, maybe odd. I had to be mature and pull myself together so we could get back to our normal. I also had to get home because I was starving. I couldn't eat much of the hospital food. In Germany, lunch is the big meal of the day, it's called the "warm meal," and it includes dishes like soups or meat with a side of potatoes, rice, or *Spätzle*, German egg noodles, which to me look like scrambled eggs. The dinner is the "cold meal" and it's made up of cold cuts and bread, and at the hospital it was no different. I was given slices of various kinds of salami, including one that was the color blood red, and rye or whole grain bread (as if the dark colored bread made the meal healthy). I just had a baby, and while it wasn't open heart surgery, everyone knows that processed meats are bad for you, especially because of the high sodium and fat content, and the preservatives.

There was also no operatic melodrama this time around because for most of my pregnancy my mother-in-law was more than 1,600 km away in Italy. She only arrived the day before I gave birth. I was also better prepared to handle unsolicited advice thanks to an episode of *Pregnancy Confidential*.[15] The hosts explained that family members, friends, and strangers who give it want to help but they may leave you questioning your decisions, and plus sometimes they're just plain annoying. There are many things you can do, including ignoring the comments, but that's not always possible with family and friends. Instead you can acknowledge them, explain the choices you've made, or gracefully change the subject. I wished I listened to the episode when I was pregnant with my daughter because I would've handled it differently. I was much more informed and grounded now thanks to podcasts.

I tried to breastfeed my son as well but when I started running into the same problems, I didn't agonize over it and decided on formula right away. I didn't care what anyone thought or said. I wasn't going through that again. I drank a lot of peppermint tea that helped with the drying up process, used the cold compresses for pain relief, and wore a super tight sports bra that felt like a cotton Lycra cage. I didn't put quark, a traditional creamy cheese much beloved in German speaking countries, on my breasts to help with the swelling as the doctor suggested. I thought it was strange to spread cheese on my breasts, no? I was released in just three days but not before getting through a lot of paperwork and bureaucracy. Even though Stolberg

---

15. Points, Dana, Turner, Chandra, and Kara Corridan, hosts. "Week 21: Weird Advice Pregnant Women Get." *Pregnancy Confidential*, Parents. Dotdash Meredith. Season 1, Episode 13, 24 Feb. 2016, parents.com/pregnancy-confidential/pregnancy-confidential-podcast-week-21-weird-advice-pregnant-women-get/

was nearby, it wasn't GK where they were accustomed to NATO military families who rented their homes and shopped on the local economy. Finally through broken English and gestures the administrative staff explained to us that our marriage certificate wasn't a long-form, international one and until we brought them an updated one the baby would take my last name, Mancini. I was elated, especially because he was taking my name — Mancini. Marco was not okay with it. He went all macho, "this is my son," on me, I've never seen him act so fast to get something done. He was ready to fly back to Italy to get the paperwork. Luckily that wasn't needed.

Things at home were also better. I was on top of it all. I was getting my daughter ready for school. I was taking care of the baby. I was going up and down our 16-step flight of stairs as if I hadn't just had a C-section. Just 10 days later, I even began to teach an eight-week college Business Writing class in the evenings at the GK base. I made the commitment to teach the course because I thought it would be good for me both emotionally and physically. Thanks to podcasts, I already knew a lot about self-care and how important it was to look after myself so that I could try to be a better individual and parent, and for those three hours each week it was fantastic to do something else. It just all worked out smoother this time around. *Danke,* Germany and podcasts.

Christmas (and a baptism) in Germany

Like many other families stationed in GK, or at least the Italian ones, when it was time to celebrate the important holidays like Christmas we packed up and went away for a few days. We went to see family, which for me meant either flying to New York or going to Naples, where most of my husband's family lives. The year my son was born, though, was different. I didn't think it was wise to travel with a two-month-old during the winter and so my husband and I decided early that we would stay local, stay home, and celebrate *Weihnachten* in GK, our first one in Germany.

I also thought it would be the perfect time to baptize my son. What better period than the one that marks the birth of Jesus Christ, the Son of God's eternal love. The timing also worked because my mother would still be here after my son's birth, and my sister and her family planned on flying over from New York. My sister was going to be my son's godmother. I also made sure my husband informed his family about our plans early on so that they too could get organized. I figured it would be easier for them, especially since they were only a short plane ride away.

I was adjusting to life with two kids, but I felt pretty good and plus it was the holidays. And because I wasn't busy organizing a family trip, I could actually see that Germans, just like the Americans and the Italians, were immensely into Christmas. I appreciated the beautiful, festive spirit I found in GK with its old-school street illuminations and the delicately adorned shop windows. I also saw lots of fresh, real trees for sale outside almost every supermarket, the norm in the United States but rare in Italy. I learned that it was

Germany that created the Christmas Tree tradition[16] in the 16th century when devout Christians brought decorated trees into their homes. It was Martin Luther who first added lighted candles to a tree after he was struck by the brilliance of twinkling stars amidst the evergreens during a walk home one winter evening. How lovely. I didn't take out our small, artificial tree that year, but instead I picked out a lovely Norwegian spruce standing almost two meters tall. I felt like I was in a Hallmark Channel Christmas movie as we drove home with it sticking out of the trunk. I love those cheesy rom coms. The tree was trimmed on the weekend after Thanksgiving, which was how we did things in the United States. The Italians waited until the 8 December, the Feast of the Immaculate Conception, to decorate. I heard that many Germans leave the tree for Christmas Eve morning. What?

I also could see that the Germans were obsessed with Advent calendars, and that their origin too is Deutsch.[17] Did they create every Christmas tradition? *Genau!* Beginning in the early 19th century, the days of advent were marked by burning a candle for the day or simply marking walls or doors with a line of chalk each day. In the early 20th century, the first printed calendars were made and later in the 1950s the calendars began to be produced on a large scale and ones filled with chocolates began to appear. I wasn't a big advent calendar person, but the choices were so plentiful that I had fun that year picking out calendars for everyone. I also, thanks to my daughter's school, learned that I needed to put out a boot (a clog in the neighboring Netherlands) outside the front door on the evening of the 5 December, which was then magically filled with chocolates and sweets for St. Nicholas' Day, the patron saint of children. This Northern European tradition was a sort of preliminary judgment of whether children were good or bad during the year.

Then, of course, there were the famous Christmas markets. I tried

---

16. "History of Christmas Trees." *History.com*. A & E Television Networks. 27 Oct. 2009, history.com/topics/christmas/history-of-christmas-trees

17. "The Advent Calendar's Sweet History." *Dw.com*. Deutsche Welle, dw.com/en/the-advent-calendars-sweet-history/g-17256886

to do some preliminary research by listening to some podcasts before I actually headed out in the cold to explore with my family. I did that regularly now, use podcasts as a research tool instead of internet search engines but I was surprised that there weren't a lot of podcasts that explored the markets in detail and how to visit them with young children. I'm usually overwhelmed by all the podcast choices, but not this time. I was thankful that Rick Steves, the American travel guru who built his company by encouraging Americans to travel to Europe, had given the markets a little space, especially since there are some 3,000 Christmas markets in Germany that attract 160 million visitors each year.[18]

In one podcast episode of Rick Steves Germany and Austria,[19] Steves spoke with two local tour guides who explained that the markets are a cultural symbol of Germany's countdown to Christmas. They spoke about the *Christkindlesmarkt* in Nuremberg, named for the Christ Child, which is traditionally represented as a female angel instead of Baby Jesus, and goes back to the time of Martin Luther, when the tradition of giving children presents at Christmas began.[20] The market is known for its opening ceremony that includes an angel, who recites a prologue to begin the festivities. The tour guides also mentioned the different markets dotted all over Berlin, some of which are more commercial, like the one at the Berlin Town Hall with its 50-meter giant Ferris wheel, and others that are more refined, like the one at the *Gendarmenmarkt,* a beautiful square that houses the German and French cathedrals and the city's concert hall. The point, they said, is that there are markets for all tastes.

These Christmas markets were too far away but I did go to Cologne, where I visited the biggest market in the city center located in front of the famous Cathedral, where there are relics of the Three

---

18. "Die wirtschaftliche Bedeutung der Volksfeste und Weihnachtsmärkte in Deutschland 2018." *Deutscher Schaustellerbund.* Report. Web. dsbev.de/fileadmin/user_upload/DSB_Studie_2018_web.pdf

19. Steves, Rick, host. "German Christmas Markets." *Rick Steves Germany and Austria*, 8 Sept. 2017, podtail.com/en/podcast/rick-steves-germany-and-austria/german-christmas-markets/

20. "Nuremberg Christkindlesmarkt." *Christkindlesmarkt.de,* christkindlesmarkt.de/en/

Kings, the Wise Men who made their way to Bethlehem bringing gold, frankincense, and myrrh. I visited the Christmas market in Aachen, also organized around the main Cathedral and the Town Hall. I also stopped at a few of the other smaller markets in the towns and villages near GK. And in the end, I decided I wasn't, don't gasp … crazy about them. I felt like I was in tipsy Christmas-themed amusement parks and I'm not a fan of amusement parks. I know almost everyone in the world thinks they are great but I don't know what all the fuss is about. I get it that the markets are about atmosphere — wooden stalls, evergreen decorations, twinkling lights, and the smell of fried food, along with cloves and cinnamon — but after a while it all became a bit nauseating. The markets were pretty much all the same to me. They all had vendors selling arts and crafts, such as glass baubles, wooden toys, knitwear, and ceramics, and most of the products weren't handmade or artisanal. There was also a lot of German market fare like roasted sweet almonds, hot chestnuts, gingerbread, and *Stollen*, a buttery fruitcake with a marzipan core and sugar-coated crust. The cake, which is supposed to resemble a swaddled Baby Jesus, is long and dense. It's good, but it's no *Panettone*, which is the Italian Christmas fruit bread, or cake, and is tall and light. The raisins and candied orange zest are not overwhelming, but carefully studded throughout. There were also more fatty foods, such as sausage, garlic bread, and deep-fried crispy potato ovals, but when I thought about the oil the vendors probably used, I quickly moved my family along. And there was the mulled wine, known as *Glühwein*, with its cinnamon, cloves, and other spices, the yummiest offering at the markets. The wine is served in a decorated, ceramic mug, which is a much-needed hand warmer, but the vendors charged a €2 or €3 extra deposit that meant you had to return the mug or you could legitimately take it home. I found it kind of hard amongst the large crowds to make my way back to our specific vendor who sold the *Glühwein*, especially since we were walking and drinking.

I also wasn't fond of the market's opening hours. Most were open on the Friday before Advent and closed on the 23 December. I've always found last minute shopping on Christmas Eve to be somewhat fun, but I guess the Germans are so organized that they leave nothing to the last minute. I wanted to sit down and have a talk with the organizing committees and tell them the markets should reopen after Christmas. I think it would be a much better marketing strategy. I knew they would attract visitors, especially since many people are off work and their kids are not in school, but instead the stalls and all the holiday decorations are being pulled down piece-by-piece. I may be a bit consumeristic but continuing to eat and shop during the week between Christmas and New Year's has always been the norm for me. In the United States and in Italy after-Christmas sales, especially on holiday items, are all the rage. Listen to me Germany!

But the biggest issue for me was that all the "fun" was happening outdoors in the freezing cold. I told you about me and the *colpo d'aria*, remember? I had three layers on when I visited the Aachen market, of which my final layer included a long down puffer coat and a super wrap-around scarf that looks like a funnel around my neck, but I couldn't warm up even after the steaming hot *Glühwein*. The air that Sunday afternoon was icy, the wind was gusting, it was especially intense at the corners and these were stalls not skyscrapers. There was no sun to offer even the slightest reprieve. I was beginning to feel uptight. I was done. I wanted to go back to the car. I wanted to go home. I had seen enough, but Marco kept stopping and looking around. I was getting annoyed with him, but he does this all the time. If we go somewhere, like a hotel, a museum, a park, or the beach, he feels like he needs to enjoy it to the fullest. I can't forget the time we brought my then six-year-old godson to DisneyLand in Florida. He was tired after several hours in Magic Kingdom Park and wanted to rest but my husband kept insisting that we go on the spinning teacup ride again, that we watch the afternoon parade, and at least wait for the evening fireworks to begin. I had to pull him aside and tell him that we needed to go, that my godson was tired, it was time to leave. Or when we went to Ischia, an island off Naples, and he insisted we stay at the beach all day, but for me the morning or the afternoon was enough. I was tired and pink from sitting in the hot sun for four hours and wanted to go back to the apartment we rented to relax in the shade. I'm more of a get-in, experience, and then get-out-type of person. I know Marco is different but still.

I was also worried about the kids at the Aachen Christmas market. I must have been out of my mind to bring them there in the cold. I had baby my son in a red snowsuit covered in a fleece blanket in the carriage, and my daughter was dressed warmly but her cheeks were bright red. I kept touching her face with my gloves to give her some warmth. My mother, who is used to cold New York, looked at me like, "What are we doing out here? *Sei impazzita?*" I'm not anti-winter or outdoor activities, even though I don't like skiing or skating, but this was not like visiting the Christmas Tree at Rockefeller Center in New York City, a holiday tradition that I've participated in and enjoyed. For me, the visit included admiring the massive tree and the holiday décor, shopping at some of the stores in the plaza, and then I would go into a warm place for drinks or food. The outdoor part ended, and I was all cozied up indoors. Even if people supposedly go to the Christmas markets to meet each other, how merry can you be if it's so cold outside? But maybe I'm just too uptight.

I was, despite my eventual bitter-cold ambivalence about the markets, happy that the holidays were here, especially because there was a lot to celebrate this year. On Christmas morning we all woke up early and the kids, including my godson who had come from New York, opened their presents and then we attended the 9:30 mass at the GK Base Chapel. The tradition after mass was to get coffee and donuts (in America) or *cornetti* (in Italy) to eat at home before we started working on preparing the meal, but that wasn't possible in GK because everything was closed. What a bummer. We went back home, made coffee, and got to work in the kitchen.

My mother led the way and prepared a traditional Italian meal that included focaccia, fried battered salted cod, cannelloni, and a crown roast of lamb, not goose, duck, or rabbit that were being sold in large numbers at the supermarkets. In addition, she had baked for a few days before the holidays. She made her simple holiday cookies shaped like bells, trees, and candy canes with red and green sprinkles, perfect for dunking in milk and coffee. She made *copeta,* a type of almond brittle with blanched whole almonds that is kept together with a blend of honey and sugar. She, more importantly, made my favorite holiday dessert *cartellate,* fried pastry spirals glazed with honey, fig syrup, or cooked grape must and sprinkled with cinnamon. They are a divine blend of stickiness and goo. They require a lot of work and once made they are treated with great care. I knew the process from when I was a little girl. The finished *cartellate* were carefully placed on a large Christmas-themed ceramic dish and first covered in plastic wrap and then aluminum foil. Then they were placed in a plastic bag and the bag's handles were tied in a knot. The dish was moved to another room, one that was dark because the *cartellate* were not to be exposed to light, and finally covered with a clean Christmas-themed tea towel. The moving back and forth of *cartellate* happened at dessert on Christmas Eve, Christmas Day, New Year's Eve, New Year's Day and any time friends or family came over for coffee during the holiday period. So we did this in our GK Christmas too. I guess we had an Italian Christmas in Germany after all.

I was able to secure the raw ingredients for most of my mother's holiday meal thanks to Guido, an Italian vendor who drives from Calabria to GK in a white, refrigerated truck filled with fruits and vegetables, fresh pasta, cheese, salami, salt cod, and other Italian goods. I learned about Guido from the Italian wives, who as I said, know everything. And he truly is a godsend because he has products in the truck that aren't available here locally. He sells broccoli rabe in the fall, artichokes in the winter, and cactus pears in the spring. I do wish he would provide a bit more notice. He sends a text message in the WhatsApp group chat called *Il Calabrese* a few hours before his arrival, stating that he will be in the parking lot behind an Italian restaurant in GK at a certain time. By the looks of it (hand trolley full of boxes going in the service entrance of the restaurant) he furnishes the restaurant as well. I go despite the short notice or if it requires me to change plans, because I don't know when he will be back again. I always feel cool when I'm standing in the line outside waiting my turn as if I'm part of a members-only group with access to exclusive products. I know, I'm ridiculous, it's just food.

With Christmas behind us it was now time to focus on my son's baptism scheduled for Sunday, 31 December, New Year's Eve. I had pretty much crossed everything off my to-do list. I had filled out the necessary paperwork at the GK Base Chapel and we had received instructions about what we needed to do during the celebration of the sacrament. In regard to dress, my sister had bought my son's baptismal outfit from The Hampton Shop, a small children's boutique on Long Island that we always shopped at for special occasions. As a young girl, my mother bought me special occasion dresses from the shop. I did, though, have to organize the final details and needed to know who from my husband's family was coming, when they were arriving, and help figure out where they were going to stay. I am an obsessive planner, but this was basic info. I asked my husband a few times, but he kept saying he didn't know yet. I didn't get it, the baptism was in a few days, and so I kept prodding him until he finally told me that no one was coming. The reason: my mother-in-law wanted my husband to organize her trip and because he hadn't (note: in the past she had organized her own trips to Germany) she wasn't coming to the baptism, and consequently neither were my two brothers-in-law and their families.

I couldn't believe she was doing this. I was sad, disappointed, and honestly pissed off. I was, however, not surprised because my mother-in-law has a history of this kind of behavior, especially when my family is around. In Italy, at my daughter's baptism, she was also upset. The problem then was that she wanted to be involved in the planning and she wasn't pleased that my sister, my best friend, and the person into whose care I would leave my kids if my husband and I were to die, was going to be my daughter's godmother. The day of the baptism was a beautiful, warm July afternoon and my mother-in-law was dressed in total black, as if she was going to a funeral.

She's often depressed during the holidays, but only the ones we don't spend with her. Every time I visit New York and we talk to her on the phone she has some kind of problem and sounds awfully sad. I understand that she's a widow and that it must be difficult, but I live far away from my family and want to enjoy them when I see them. I sometimes think that her problem is with me. Is it because I took her son away? Is it because we never lived in Naples? Is it because we now live in another country? Elena, my sister-in-law who has been in the family for more than 25 years, said there is no one explanation. She also has a long list of melodramas in which my mother-in-law had a starring role. For example, she was upset when Elena and Marco's oldest brother Lorenzo decided to buy a home in a small town located on the slopes of Mt. Vesuvius. She thought it was too dangerous, imagining another Pompeii. I told you, drama! Elena does say that I'm lucky because my mother-in-law is now older, a bit weaker, and that she was stronger and feistier when she was younger. I can only imagine.

As the baptism approached, I kept telling myself that I wasn't going to let my mother-in-law affect us. I wasn't going to let her ruin the day. But it wasn't quite working. I could see my husband was sad and upset, even somewhat embarrassed by his family. I understood, but I wanted to shake him a lot. I wanted him to stop sulking. Some of my family members were here, they had spent money on transatlantic flights and he was acting like a baby. I had to focus on his feelings, and it wasn't fair, especially on this day. I thought he was really immature. Finally, I did manage to get through to him and we were able to enjoy at least in some measure what was a beautiful occasion. The ceremony at the chapel was simple. My son wore a white, long sleeve romper with three satin button accents and matching shoes. His small head was covered with a fine knit beanie, and he was draped in the white, basketweave stitch crocheted blanket my mother made. In the evening, we celebrated my son and New Year's Eve with a small group of Italian families that had also oddly stayed in GK for the holidays. I socialized a bit; can you believe it? I had my mother and sister there for support, they are different from me, they are friendly and like talking to people. I'm more like my father, a bit standoffish at least at first. We gathered at the Chapel's annex with homemade dishes — my mother thankfully took charge again and prepared lasagna and meatloaf and roasted potatoes. There was some spread that night and there was a happy vibe, which was exactly what I needed to feel that night, not resentment towards my mother-in-law who hadn't even called to congratulate us.

Two days later I drove my family to the airport. The saying goodbye part hasn't become any easier over the years, instead it only seems harder as I get older and have become more sensitive about things. I cry a lot more easily now. Later at home with everyone gone and my husband back at work, my daughter back in school, I began to obsess over what had happened with my mother-in-law. I needed to put it to rest. I had in the past come across some advice about forgiveness in a parenting podcast[21] that I listened to once in a while called *Happiness Matters Podcast*.

I found the podcast by chance while I was on the website of the online magazine called *Greater Good* from the University of California, Berkeley, which features lots of stories about leading a healthier life. The hosts Dr. Christine Carter and Registered Nurse Rona Renner said the old adages of "forgive and forget," or "turn a blind eye" aren't the most helpful and are actually quite misleading. I am glad somebody finally said this. The only way to move through a negative feeling is to identify it and understand why it causes you pain, and only then can you come to terms with what has happened. They said, moreover, that the forgiveness part is something that we do for ourselves not for the person or people we are forgiving, it's all about making ourselves happier. The duo stressed in the episode how important it was to help your kids with the process, but I found that their suggestions were on target for me as well. I was hurt, again, by my mother-in-law's actions but I forgave her because it wouldn't help me or my relationship with Marco to be filled with resentment. I'm full of flaws and insecurities but I'm not mean. I haven't, though, forgotten. I get flashbacks occasionally, but I work hard at pushing them aside, like the podcast hosts said, it should be more like "forgive and let go."

I wanted my mother-in-law to apologize. I would have appreciated it. I wished she could have listened to an Italian version of the *Happier with Gretchen Rubin* podcast episode about saying sorry,[22] and how it's an important step when it comes to repairing relationships. I enjoyed this podcast not only for its content — how to make life better — but also because happiness guru Gretchen Rubin hosts the show with her sister Elizabeth Craft, a TV writer and producer based out of Los Angeles. I'm an ambassador of the sisterhood bond, and after I

---

21. Renner, Rona and Christine Carter, hosts. "Forgive and Forget." *Happiness Matters Podcast,* 10 May 2012. greatergood.berkeley.edu/podcasts/item/forgive_and_forget

22. Rubin, Gretchen, host. "Say "I'm Sorry," an Interview with Hollywood Legend Sherry Lansing, and a Spice-Related Hack." *Happiness with Gretchen Rubin,* Episode 114, 26 April 2017. gretchenrubin.com/podcast-episode/podcast-114-happier-sherry-lansing

listened to the show, I always think about how fun it would be to chat it up with my sister on a podcast. I think we are cool. I know, it's not cool to think or say you're cool. The episode focused on the languages of apology outlined in a 2006 book called *The Five Languages of Apology* by authors Gary Chapman and Jennifer Thomas. They are: 1. Expressing regret – "I'm sorry" 2. Accepting responsibility – "I was wrong" 3. Making restitution – "What can I do to make it right?" 4. Genuinely repenting – "I'll try not to do that again" 5. Requesting forgiveness – "Will you please forgive me?" I felt like my mother-in-law's apology for trying to ruin my son's baptism should be a combination of numbers one, two, and four. I thought Marco's apology for sulking and being immature should be a combination of two and three. I received a half apology from Marco. I received no apology whatsoever from my mother-in-law, instead she just pretended it all never happened. For me, though, it was a Christmas and Baptism to remember. The following Christmas we packed up and went to Naples. She obviously did not wear black.

Trying to worry less, parent more

My husband says I am *pesante* when it comes to the kids, which translates to heavy, but what it actually means is that I'm hard to take. I don't think I am. I'm just a little hyper-protective. I pay close attention to what my kids are doing and what they are putting into their minds and bodies. I only do this because I love them. I worry about them. My rules, right?

I do sometimes wish I could turn my mind off and stop what is often counterproductive worrying. Are they going to hurt themselves on the trampoline? (I still can't understand why my husband bought it.) Have they eaten a balanced Mediterranean diet (Did that meal have whole grains, veggies, and fruit to help them poop?). But it's no good. I can't switch off. It doesn't help that Marco's job here in GK includes deployments to far-away countries. The deployments can be for weeks or even months, and that means I'm alone in GK with the kids. Who wouldn't be *pesante* in this situation? I'm sometimes annoyed with Marco for putting me in this predicament. I often communicate to him my frustration and fatigue. Is that immature? Is it hurting our marriage? I don't know, but what I do know is that in Italy I spoke the language and had Marco's family if I needed anything, and he was always around. In Germany, I don't speak the language and like I said I don't have family and much of a network of friends that I can turn to, and I'm often going at it alone like a single parent.

I pray a lot. I pray that Marco is safe (especially because every time he leaves, he reminds me of his life insurance policy), but also that me and the kids are okay and make it through this period without any major illnesses or injuries. I sleep terribly when he's away. I also help myself with information and lots of support from parenting podcasts mostly hosted by moms. The topics include everything like friendships, bilingualism, vitamins, and table manners. I find myself reflecting not only on what the hosts are saying but revisiting my own personal experiences. Parenting podcasts make me feel like I'm part of something, a community of parents who worry about their kids as much as me. Yes, there are other people out there that get it and get me.

The challenging part was sorting through hundreds of parenting podcasts to find ones that I wanted to listen to and that worked for me. I don't regularly listen to the most popular or best ranked parenting podcasts, such as *The Longest Shortest Time*, and *Care and Feeding* (once called *Mom and Dad are Fighting*). I skip them, but not because I'm trying to engage in group polarization or be rebellious. I'm not like that. I just wanted podcasts with great content that aren't so mainstream; that way maybe they'll be a little exclusive to me. I like being an insider, and the right podcast offers that opportunity. I also skip parenting podcasts filled with child psychology talk like *Practical Intuition with Kay* and *Your Parenting Mojo*. I respect what the hosts are trying to do but I tend to lose focus and my mind starts to wander when they use jargon.

I did find and get wrapped up in listening to *The Mom Hour*, a podcast hosted by Meagan Francis, a mother of five from Michigan, and Sarah Powers, a mother of three from California. I respect these women just for the sheer number of children between them! The podcast, which has been around since 2016, is not an interview-based show but one overflowing conversation. I didn't know where to start and didn't feel I could just jump in and listen to the latest episode, especially since I needed a deep breath when I found more than 200 episodes available. I am telling you that's a lot to sort through. I visited their website and found a section for new listeners. I started there with "The Life Changing Habit of Opting Out."[23] They talked and laughed a lot, for some 60 minutes, about opting out of things without feeling guilty, including not sending photo Christmas cards (I like showing off my kids!), doing homework in Kindergarten and 1st

---

23. Francis, Meagan and Sarah Powers, hosts. "The Life-Changing Magic of Opting Out." *The Mom Hour*, Life Listened, Episode 161, 19 June 2018. themomhour.com/161/

Grade (Is that allowed?) and not folding pajamas (I could never do that — a dresser drawer that looks like one giant mess would definitely give me more anxiety…)

I did connect with opting out of kids' birthday parties. I started thinking about all the parties I have grudgingly gone to since we moved to Germany, ughhhhh. On average, I think we've been invited to at least 15 birthday parties a year. The parties are not hosted at home with chips, ice cream, and games like Pin the Tail on the Donkey, from when I was a kid (that was so much fun). They are now mostly held at giant indoor playgrounds. I figure this is a Northern European thing because I'm often going to these parties in Germany and the Netherlands. I guess because it rains a lot or maybe I have just been out of the birthday-party loop for a while. I don't know, but I hate these places, and if I mention this to other parents, they immediately look disappointed, as if I said, "I hate puppies." I don't send my kids willingly. I have never organized an afternoon at one of them because I wanted my kids to have fun and play. They can just play in our backyard or entertain themselves; I did that when I was little. I also don't like the fact that I sometimes have to sign a waiver, excluding the property owners from any responsibility if my child gets hurt. I told you, these places are dangerous! Plus, there are viruses and germs lurking everywhere. They say they clean the plastic-colored balls and the ropes, which the kids jump into and use to climb, but I don't believe they do. The fact is every time I go to one of these playgrounds my kids get sick or injured and I then promise myself that we will never go again.

My daughter's friend's mother sent an email invitation to her son's seventh birthday party and guess where it was – an indoor playground called Grimmdome across the Dutch-German border. I had surprisingly never been to a party at Grimmdome, but the name already sounded dark and germy. I said to myself, "No, she's not going. I'll make up an excuse." The mother of the birthday boy, a French national married to an Italian stationed in GK, was going through a divorce and she mentioned that she wasn't sure her son's father would even attend the party. She was even more of an outsider with the wives. I felt bad and caved, and later responded with "Yes, we'll be there!" She said I could also bring my son, I said "no, don't worry" — there was no way my son was going too. The two-hour party started promptly at noon. The kids were first seated at a long table with balloons and served chicken nuggets and fries, which they hardly ate, and then ran into the big play area that was already filled with children, but not the ones from our party. I found it hard to keep track of my daughter (I do worry about kidnappings) and so I was also running around this giant playground watching her and her shoeless (yuck!) friends. I almost died when I saw kids there who were sockless. A number of parents decided to drop off their kids and pick them up later — how nice. My daughter finally slowed down when she hurt her arm and needed an ice pack. Then another friend from her class bumped her knee, another ice pack, and another friend got a bloody nose, tissues galore. This was a two-hour party on a Sunday, the day of rest. I went home and had to disinfect her — "don't touch anything, get undressed and get straight in the shower." I threw her socks in the garbage; I wasn't putting them in my washing machine. Then she started feeling ill and by midnight she was sick with a fever. Was it the playground party? Guess what I think?

I wish I had listened to the episode before Grimmdome, but now I'm done saying yes to anything involving indoor playgrounds. I don't have to feel guilty, "it's okay, not to do lots of things," the podcast's hosts said. I don't need to. I have to put my needs first, and they were adamant about it. The podcast's hosts, as I mentioned earlier, live in different parts of the United States and they often acknowledge the challenges of parenting in different places with different cultures. I get it, I'm trying to raise my kids in Germany, right near the Dutch border, and her friends who are from many different NATO countries, have different ways of doing things. Sure, I can't confide my apprehensions nor my preferences with them, but I still have to do what's good for us. Thank you, podcaster Meaghan and podcaster Sara, my fellow American mommies.

I often listen to the hour-long *The Mom Hour* episodes while I wait for my daughter's Italian class to finish — she studies Italian once a week for 90 minutes. The class is preparing her for her eventual return to Italian school, which I imagine will be painfully difficult for her (and me). I can usually fit in two episodes during the wait if I cut through part of the introduction and if I increase the playback speed (yes, you can do that with podcasts). When I listened to the episode "Helping Kids with Doctor Visits, Shots and Appointment Fear"[24] I remembered what happened when I brought my kids to our doctor's office for their annual influenza vaccine. Drama! In Germany, public health insurance only covers the vaccine for children with underlying health issues, and so most local parents skip this one. I don't, I follow the U.S. Centers for Disease Control recommendation[25] and I get my kids vaccinated. I've read horror stories about kids dying from the flu. Another worry. I asked my doctor for a script, ordered the vaccines, paid for them, picked them up at the pharmacy, and brought them to the doctor's office in a small cooler bag. This was the process, it was quite laborious, but I didn't have any other options. In the U.S. everything is done at the pediatrician's office, no ordering or picking up the vaccines, no cooler bags for transport. Plus, you can also get vaccinated at your local pharmacy. Back in Italy, my pediatrician's office didn't handle vaccinations. I was sent to the local public health office where all vaccinations were done.

Now in Germany, I expected my baby son to squirm and cry a little, but I would just hold him and it would be done quickly. I knew my daughter didn't like getting shots, but we talked about it. I prepped her and assured her it was going to be fast and that she would only feel a little pinch. I also bribed her. I promised her an L.O.L. surprise, the big-headed, millennial-inspired fashion dolls with names like Miss Independent and Touchdown Baby Confetti Pop. I bought one and it was in the car on the way to the doctor's office. I even showed it to her before we got out and said, "It's all yours, just get the shot, and then you can open it!" I thought this was a pretty smart move, and plus I would reward her for being brave. I arrived and went in with both kids, hand-in-hand. The young, stoic assistant at my German pediatrician's office, who spoke English well, asked who would go

---

24. Francis, Meagan and Sarah Powers, hosts. "Helping Kids With Doctor Visits, Shots, and 'Appointment Fear.'" *The Mom Hour*, Life Listened, Episode 180, 30 Oct. 2018, themomhour.com/180/

25. "Flu & Young Children." *U.S. Centers for Disease Control and Prevention*, 25 Oct. 2021, cdc.gov/flu/highrisk/children.htm

first. I said, "My daughter!" She panicked, tried to run out of the room, cried hysterically, and screamed, "no, no, no." I pointed towards the car — the doll was in there — but it wouldn't calm her down. Then my son started crying because his sister was crying, "the blood bond, not now," I thought. I was completely embarrassed. I wanted to run out of there. The assistant gently removed my screaming son from the room, but I could still hear him. I started to get a little loud too and yell and told my daughter that "this wasn't okay!" She needed to be brave; it was no big deal. Finally, after 10 minutes of this, I got her to sit down, and with some force and threats she was vaccinated.

My wise podcast hosts assured me that shots are non-negotiables, and that this kind of behavior is normal for apprehensive kids everywhere. The doctor's office was turned upside down by our presence that day. The holding down, the bribing, "Team Bribe" as the podcast hosts call it, are also okay (thanks, for saying that!) in the case of shots because sometimes "you just have to get through it." I didn't get any clear advice or suggestions for what I needed to do the next time, but the podcast doesn't always tell listeners what to do. I think in this case they just want moms to feel like they are supported, that they have been there too. I felt that way. I started listening to newly released episodes, which in addition to their weekly conversation also includes an extra monthly episode in which they talk to expert financial advisors, pediatricians, child psychologists, authors, other podcasters. I like what they are doing in their one, big conversation. I like that they cut back on the comparisons and instead talk about what worked or didn't work for them.

I also found a podcast called *Comfort Food* that helped me stress less about what my kids are and are not eating. I do blame Marco and his food-obsessed family for my current fixation because all they think about is food. I was much more laidback before I met him, at least from a fruit and vegetable perspective. The podcast, which started in 2018 and went on "hiatus" in 2020, is hosted by mothers and food writers Amy Palanjian and Virginia Sole-Smith. They are not the smoothest talkers and sometimes they fumble over words, but they sound like normal people, normal moms. I liked that they worried and agonized over food related things, just like me. I picked the weekly episodes of the podcast that I listened to depending on what was going on in my life and with my kids, and also because the episodes are quite long, in the 30–50-minute range. I've skipped many, like Episode 6. "Eating While Pregnant;" that's never happening again, next. Also, Episode 37, "How The Heck to Start Milk Weaning;" done with that, pass. Episode 13 and 49. "How To Stop Freaking Out About Halloween Candy;" I'm not, next.

I have, thanks to Marco, always done food with my kids the Italian way. In Italy, my daughter's pediatrician, Dr. Romano, told me to start preparing food for her at eight months. I thought he was going to say to start her off with some baby carrots and peas, but no, he wanted me to make her a meal from scratch. I was like, "I can't just give her some jar food to start?" No. I needed to cook. I pulled out my notebook from my bag and started taking notes, as if I was getting facts for a story I was writing. I'm sure Dr. Romano thought I was a strange American woman, but I didn't have much experience with babies and in the kitchen. I was instructed to make a big pot of vegetable soup. Then I was told to take some of the broth, puree a vegetable from it, add some rice cereal, extra virgin olive oil, and grated *parmigiano* cheese, aged at least 30 months, and mix it all together. I thought this was crazy. Olive oil and *parmigiano*, for an eight-month-old! I asked a lot of questions and that's when Dr. Romano decided to write it all down for me. I had it all down in my notebook, but I took his notes anyway. I went home and reluctantly started putting this meal together, and surprise, surprise my daughter liked it and ate so much of it during the weaning period.

In Germany, they gave me little to no instruction about how to start weaning my son. The pediatrician's assistant oversaw this part of my visit which was unimportant to the doctor (gasp), and she casually said to pick up some baby food and try it all out — that's it. What? That's it? Yes. I looked at jarred food on the shelves of the *Drogerie*, which is basically a retail store selling beauty, hygiene, and household related products, sort of like CVS Health but without the pharmacy component. The choices were odd, pureed spaghetti Bolognese, salmon with potatoes, and couscous with vegetables. I was mortified and went the Italian route with my son as well.

But as my kids are getting older, they are getting pickier and

Palanjian and Sole-Smith have given me some new perspective like in the episode "What To Do About Snacking."[26] For a while I was trying not to give my kids snacks in the afternoon. I wasn't sure if that was good or bad, but I knew that if my kids were really really hungry then they wouldn't give me trouble at dinner. The whole meal was easier, they ate whatever I prepared — pasta with lentils, broccoli and rice, even squash and potatoes. I did feel somewhat bad when they asked for something or were pulling on the refrigerator door and I said "no, no, you'll eat later." The episode, however, helped me to rethink my snack strategy. I learned that my little-to-no snack rule was probably not the best and that kids need snacks between their big meals. I thought that was just for dieting adults so they would eat less. I let them open the refrigerator now.

And the episode "Is it OK for Kids to Drink Chocolate Milk?"[27] reinforced my prejudice against sugary drinks. My daughter loves chocolate milk and I always felt like I was giving her a sugar fix. I listened to the hosts talk about new guidelines for children from Healthy Eating Research,[28] a Robert Wood Johnson Foundation program, that said all little ones under five-years-old should avoid drinking flavored milks, along with plant-based or non-dairy milks, and even juice. Oh crap, my daughter is drinking this up. The podcast hosts tried to argue that chocolate milk has protein and carbs, which are good for kids, but after the episode, I cut down on my daughter's chocolate milk intake by throwing out our chocolate drink mix in the trash. If it's not in the house anymore she can't have it, right?

And while I like Palanjian and Sole-Smith, I didn't always agree

---

26. Palanjian, Amy and Virginia Sole-Smith, hosts. "What To Do About Snacking (And Why Your Kid Doesn't Want to Eat Meals)." *Comfort Food*, Episode 38, 15 Aug. 2019, comfortfoodpodcast.libsyn.com/38-what-to-do-about-kid-snack-culture

27. Palanjian, Amy and Virginia Sole-Smith, hosts. "Is it OK for Kids to Drink Chocolate Milk?" *Comfort Food*, Episode 46, 10 Oct.. 2019. comfortfoodpodcast.libsyn.com/46-is-it-ok-for-kids-to-drink-chocolate-milk

28. "Leading Health Organizations Support First-Ever Consensus Recommendations to Encourage Young Children's Consumption of Healthy Drinks." *Healthy Eating Research*, 18 Sept. 2019, healthyeatingresearch.org/wp-content/uploads/2019/09/HER-HealthyBeverage-Press-Release.pdf. Press Release.

with them and follow their advice. They have gripes with things, including *The Berenstain Bears*, the children's book series about a family of bears. The bears, in particular the children, Brother Bear and Sister Bear, learn a heartfelt lesson at the end of each story. I read the books when I was young, and they are a positive childhood memory. The hosts said Mama and Papa Bear do a lot of "moral policing," have too many rules, and label things, including food as good and bad, which they believe hurts kids. I do that too. I don't think it's wrong! In the podcast episode "Kids-In-Restaurant Survival Guide,"[29] they pointed to *Go out to Eat* where they say Mama Bear "micromanaged" the whole meal telling her kids they couldn't have French fries and instead had to eat all their broccoli before they could have dessert. Is there something wrong with that? I like *The Berenstain Bears* and read them out loud to my kids. For me they are a good tool to help teach some life lessons and even introduce touchy subjects. My daughter was a little frightened after we read *Learn About Strangers* but that's what I wanted. I wanted her to be cautious, and yes afraid of people she doesn't know.

I also really liked the *Good Kids (How Not To Raise an A**hole)* podcast. I was attracted to it, well, because of its name. I definitely don't want to raise 'a**holes.' I fear children like that. I don't like kids who are rude and impolite to people, to parents, to family members. I don't want assholes and unfortunately sometimes my kids do asshole-type things and I'm mortified and embarrassed.

From the small podcast network Lemonada Media, the podcast has helped me to stop some asshole behavior and raise "kinder, gentler humans." The podcast begins each episode with a disclaimer about its language, noting that it's not for little ears, especially since words like "asshole," "fuck," "dumbass," and "butthead" are often part of the vocabulary. But after the disclaimer, the podcast doesn't have much of an order except the fact that they talk about how to raise a good kid. There is no single host. They have a guest host or hosts each episode, who often include important parenting

---

29. Palanjian, Amy and Virginia Sole-Smith, hosts. "The Kids-In-Restaurants Survival Guide" *Comfort Food*, Episode 32, 18 April. 2019, comfortfoodpodcast.libsyn.com/32-the-kids-in-restaurants-survival-guide

personalities that I'm happy to hear from, such as Nora McInerny, who writes about grief and loss and hosts the *Terrible, Thanks for Asking* podcast, and DeRay McKesson, a former schoolteacher and administrator turned activist and now host of *Pod Save the People*. There also is no recurring frequency of when new episodes will be available. They debuted with five episodes in November 2019, then released another episode after two weeks, then dropped another episode one week later, then another two episodes a few days later. A bit confusing, yes. The podcast's lack of a structured frequency is disappointing for someone like me who thrives on order and organization. The one thing the podcast does is ensure that it doesn't take up too much of my time — episodes are only about 15 minutes each. I listen to them in their entirety and can invest the time even if the specific topic isn't relevant to me at the moment.

I was taken from the very first episode with the title "How To Make Your Kids Say Thank You. And Mean it"[30] in which Jaime Primak Sullivan, a mom and reality television star told the story of how in 2016 her three kids went into Dairy Queen, ordered their ice cream and ran out without saying "thank you" and acknowledging the employee who served them. She was upset, felt defeated, and questioned whether her parenting skills were up to par. I've felt like that many times. She asked whether her kids were "good people or are they just little shits who have been given too much?" I've asked myself that many times too. She took their ice cream and threw it in the garbage, and they whined, complained, and they called her the "meanest mom ever," But she talked to them about the importance of the words "please" and "thank you" and about connecting with people.

I hated that my daughter often shied away from saying "hello" or "thank you" to people. She said she was embarrassed and often hid behind me. I understood it up until she was three years old but became annoyed by it. When I was her age, I was expected to say hello and greet every single person — family member or friend —

---

30. Primak Sullivan, Jaime, host. "How to Make your Kids say Thank You. And Mean it." *Good Kids*, 26 Nov. 2019, omny.fm/shows/good-kids/how-to-make-your-kids-say-thank-you-and-mean-it-wi

that entered my home or that I visited with a kiss on the cheek. I also said "thank you" to everyone, it was like a vocal reflex, a door opened, thank you; a cookie given to me, thank you; a book borrowed, thank you; my mother engrained the two words in my vocabulary. I thought, while I was listening, "I need my daughter to step it up." I don't want her to look through people and not say "hello" to them. I want her to be well-mannered. I don't care if she is embarrassed, enough now. I sat her down later and we had a real conversation about it, not the angry one I was usually having in the car after she avoided saying hello to somebody. We agreed that she would say "hello" to people and if she was uncomfortable kissing them on the cheek, she would give air kisses. Italians do a double-cheek kiss. I did this in Italy. Italians in America do a single-cheek kiss. I did this in New York. Germans don't kiss, they do a firm handshake with eye contact. To me, all are acceptable in their place.

In another episode of *Good Kids* Jamilah Lemieux, best known for hosting the podcast *Mom and Dad are Fighting,* which shares the triumphs and failures of parenting, guest hosted and talked about listening and engaging children so parents can help them make better decisions in the long run and therefore end up as "good kids."[31] I was happy to hear her as a guest host. She said parents shouldn't act like police officers, but instead should be a guiding force. "We are spiritual advisers. We are doctors and healers and teachers," Lemieux said. And I was like, "Yes, me too, I'm those things to my kids." At least, I pray I am. Like many parents she found herself sounding like a broken record repeating the same things over and over to her daughter and sometimes offering little more than "because I said so." I also use — "I'm in charge," "I'm the mommy, and you have to listen to me," and "You are doing what I say." She said these declarative phrases mean basically nothing to children (I thought these were great, powerful one-liners, what?) and what children really need is dialogue and explanation. Lemieux added: "So for me to hear my child means that I have to abandon the idea that I am the all-seeing

---

31. Lemieux, Jamilah, host. "How to Raise An Emotionally Intelligent Child." *Good Kids,* 10 Dec. 2019, omny.fm/shows/good-kids/how-to-raise-an-emotionally-intelligent-child-with

eye, that I am the beginning of the end of what is right and moral and correct in our home, and affirming that she is also a person with thoughts and ideas and sometimes her thoughts ideas make more sense than my own, or will inform the way I operate going forward, if I simply take the time to hear them out."

I swallowed hard, twisted my mouth a bit during and after this episode. I do the "I'm in charge" thing a lot, a whole lot. I know I could be more patient, explain more to my daughter and son, even if I feel like I have answered their questions 100 times already. I feel like my daughter always has questions at bedtime and I tend to be short with her. I tell her "no more talking," and "you need to go to bed." I thought it was more of a strategy on her part to stay awake then to get educated on various odd topics like endangered animals and the solar system. I want to raise good kids, not assholes, so I took Lemieux's points and did something with them. I decided to try and be more "calm, patient, thoughtful and engaged," and so when my daughter asks questions at bedtime, I don't dismiss them, at least not immediately. I answer them quickly and then tell her to go to bed. Better, right?

I also listened to the podcast *Mom Brain* because I thought it was fun and hip. The podcast made motherhood feel sophisticated, unlike stereotypical mom things, like minivans, power walking, and wearing workout gear to drop off/pick up your kids at school. The interview-driven podcast was hosted by Hilaria Baldwin, a former yoga instructor married to actor Alec Baldwin with seven kids, and Daphane Oz, a television personality who also has four kids. They often interviewed one guest and then used their own personal stories, ideas, and opinions to round out the show. They laughed a lot and even cried showing the range of emotions that we moms go through. I admired that Baldwin and Oz didn't play it safe with their often-high profile guests and that their guests don't play it safe with them (or at least they don't edit out).

In one episode designer Rebecca Minkoff, a mother of three, talked about how she delivered all of her children 'naturally' without an epidural.[32]

She was proud and cited statistics to support her belief that epidurals lead to cesarean sections. She mentioned how women have been delivering children without help for 10,000 years. But Baldwin, who had several epidurals, asked her, "Would you have a tooth pulled without anesthesia?" Or in another episode[33] when Julie Morgenstern, an organization and productivity expert, talked about how to get a pantry or bedroom in order and Baldwin said she first buys the bins or baskets she needs and then sorts the items, Morgenstern said "that's shopping," not organizing, explaining that it makes more sense to create the order first and then buy the right amount and size of containers needed. I also liked that *Mom Brain* included men in the mix of guests, which you don't get from many parenting podcasts. In one episode they chatted with Adam Grant,[34] a psychologist and professor at the Wharton School of the University of Pennsylvania known for his studies on how human beings find motivation and meaning. In another episode they talked with Dr. Dan Siegel,[35] a neuropsychiatrist best known for his 2011 book *The Whole-Brain Child* and discussed the importance of present parenting and building valuable relationships. They laughed with these guests too despite the more serious context (it's one thing when you talk to a designer and another when you talk to a doctor) but they asked good questions and brought some delicate issues into the spotlight.

---

32. Baldwin, Hilaria, and Daphne Oz, hosts. "Vagina Therapy With Rebecca Minkoff." *Mom Brain*, Gallery Group Originals, 9 Oct. 2018, art19.com/shows/mom-brain/episodes/a54b86e8-6862-4d76-a52a-cc2ad316c920

33. Baldwin, Hilaria, and Daphne Oz, hosts. "Finding Order In The Chaos with Julie Morgenstern!" *Mom Brain*, Gallery Group Originals, 15 Jan. 2020, art19.com/shows/mom-brain/episodes/6d0ab7e9-54a5-4998-962a-1954725e7357/embed

34. Baldwin, Hilaria, and Daphne Oz, hosts. "Teaching Our Kids Meaning, Generosity, and Originality With Adam Grant." *Mom Brain*, Gallery Group Originals, 31 Oct. 2018, art19.com/shows/mom-brain/episodes/41f8c25b-e65b-4eda-b8da-80bf68e4047d

35. Baldwin, Hilaria, and Daphne Oz, hosts. "Teaching Our Kids Mindsight and Fostering Their Internal Compass With Dr. Dan Siegel." *Mom Brain*, Gallery Group Originals, 18 Dec. 2019, art19.com/shows/mom-brain/episodes/9998cd02-caa7-4610-b5ac-a873cdab5bf6

The episodes of *Mom Brain* end with Baldwin and Oz talking about their favorite things, products, or services that they love or are into at the moment. I was duped and bought some of the products they talked about, including the chia bars and eye drops. I also had a ton of reservations.

In one episode when actress Alysia Reiner[36] explained that her daughter was really into her library card and said that "if you develop a reader, first of all you never need a toy." I was like, "okay, whose kid is this?" I love reading and books and so do my kids, but wow! Then when she added that her then nine-year-old daughter spends five hours on the weekend reading, I was again diffident…what? Baldwin noted that when she's in a library she thinks magically about how many people have touched a book and entered into the story. I think, "Eww, there must be germs all over this book." I read the library books my daughter brings home from school each week and then I wash my hands and tell my daughter to as well.

---

36. Baldwin, Hilaria, and Daphne Oz, hosts. "Actress Alysia Reiner Talks About Open And Honest Communication With Our Kids." *Mom Brain*, Gallery Group Originals, 2 Jan. 2019. art19.com/shows/mom-brain/episodes/1192b40d-4fd2-45a0-9846-18bff6c9fc0b

Skimming in my 40s

Ever since I moved to GK, I began thinking a lot more about aging, about getting old (long exasperated sighs here). The World Health Organization[37] says aging results from the impact of the accumulation of a wide variety of molecular and cellular damage over time. It leads to a gradual decrease in physical and mental capacity, a growing risk of disease, and ultimately death. I don't want to age or be aging. I don't want to be in this phase ever, but it was happening here in Germany. I was getting closer to the big 4-0 and it was starting to weigh on me.

I turned 40 when my son was only 10 months old and my husband thought it would be great to celebrate three times — before, on, and after the blessed day. I was in New York in August, my birthday month, and I had an early birthday dinner with my family at a waterfront restaurant on the Patchogue River, right off the Great South Bay. I chose a seafood place because I often long for it — there isn't a seafood shop in GK and the surrounding area. I wore an off the shoulder, white dress and with the sea breeze blowing through my fresh balayage highlight — my New York hairdresser David covered up all my grays and whites — I devoured tuna tartar, seared calamari, and fish tacos. I also had a chocolate cannoli cream filled cake from Mario's, the Italian bakery my family uses for special occasions, with "Happy Birthday Rosey" written in pink, my favorite color, but the giant "40" candle on it was painful to look at. Later on the day of my birthday, 31 August, I was back in Germany and went out for dinner in the Netherlands at a brasserie housed in the Rolduc Abbey complex that dates back to the 12th century. The structure and the

---

37. "Ageing and Health." The World Health Organization, 4 Oct. 2021, www.who.int/news-room/fact-sheets/detail/ageing-and-health

grounds are lovely, and the food was okay. I again dressed the birthday girl part, but this time a somber black dress with a gray shawl (colors that I look terrible in because I have skin with warm undertones). I looked like I was going to a funeral, the only thing I needed was a bouquet of lilies. Then when the waiter asked what the occasion was, I wanted to run and hide in the on-site chapel. Later at home with one kid on each side I blew out another "40" candle. Finally, during the weekend, my husband invited over a few of his colleagues and their families for a birthday barbeque — burger, ribs, and of course bratwurst. I didn't know these people well, but they were nice enough to come and they even brought me flowers. I had another cake and used the same "40" candle on it and my husband insisted everyone sing, but this time my son was crying, more like screaming hysterically. I couldn't calm him down. I felt overwhelmed and old. I felt like the geriatric mom that I was by definition, a mature older mom. I wanted this birthday to be over with.

    I turned to my podcasts to help me with all this age anxiety. I was able to neutralize some of these agonizing thoughts with the *Skimm This* podcast which transported me to a younger and hipper world. From American news media company theSkimm, which first made a name for itself with its daily morning newsletter, the podcast covered the week's most important news stories in a chic self-indulgent type of way. The target audience: millennials, anyone born between 1981 and 1996, in particular millennial women. The average 20-minute episodes not only helped me get updated about the news, but it also made me feel like I was using a plumping lip gloss.

    The structure of this potent podcast was simple. Each episode usually covered about three or four stories, with one being a big national or international piece of news. The other news seemed to be retrofitted to millennial interests with subjects, such as politics, climate change, education, poverty, religious conflict, and pop culture. The podcast often ended with an upbeat item where listeners learn about something light — Facebook's new dating service or Amazon Prime Day's kick off. The stories and their content were all explained in a lighthearted way. For example, the International Monetary Fund (IMF) was defined as "like a big, financial club" and the U.S. government lending agencies Fannie Mae and Freddie Mac were described as "not your grandparents' pet names for each other." This approach may seem too juvenile for someone supposedly mature like me, but this podcast energized me. Plus, it was easy to multitask when I listened to *Skimm This*. I could make three beds and fold/put away at least two loads of laundry per episode.

The *Skimm This* podcast had a range of different hosts, or voices to lead the way, but the thing they all had in common is that they sound like the podcast's target audience — millennials. They didn't have deep, authoritative voices but sounded young, upbeat, and ready to take on the world. They sounded happy to be telling their listeners what's going on out there in the big world. I pictured them as youthful Nora Ephrons wearing Free People clothing and Vans sneakers. Their linguistic style included speaking super, super fast and using acronyms like FOMO (fear of missing out), OMG (oh my God), LOL (laugh out loud), and K (okay). This was combined with upspeak, also known as uptalk, rising inflection or high rising intonation, in which pitch increases at the end of the sentence. Their voices had elements of vocal fry, a specific sound quality caused by the movement of the vocal cords. They ended their sentences with a sort of sizzle and/or gasp. I even heard some Valspeak, which is a dialect spoken by California girls from the San Fernando Valley.

This linguistic style is controversial, especially since it's often associated with female speakers. The women who use it have been the targets of jokes and criticism. In an episode of one of *Slate's* language podcasts *Spectacular Vernacular* (at the time called *Lexicon Valley*)[38] Bob Garfield called the style "vulgar," "annoying," and "repulsive." He called his daughter to the microphone during the episode to mimic the speech pattern. "Ida be obnoxious," he said. I disagree. I like the upspeak buzz. I like its youthfulness and energy. I like its bright colorful tones. In 2015, feminist author Naomi Wolf

---

38. Garfield Bob, and Mike Vuolo, hosts. "Get Your Creak On." *Spectacular Vernacular*, Episode 24, 2 Jan. 2013, podcasts.apple.com/ie/podcast/lexicon-valley-24-get-your-creak-on/id500673866?i=1000127462710

added to the controversy[39] when she implored millennial women to get rid of their vocal fry or risk not being taken seriously. For Wolf, ending a declarative statement — "Today is Monday" — on a high note typically reserved for questions — "Is it Monday?" — betrays a speaker's lack of confidence and a willingness to defer to their interlocutor. She wrote that what was "heartbreaking" about this female voice was that it was happening to the most transformational generation of young women in history. However, Dr. Penny Eckert, Professor of Linguistics at Stanford University, explained that attitudes toward vocal fry, upspeak, and other ways of talking are generational. In a podcast episode of *NPR's* radio program *Fresh Air*,[40] Eckert admitted that she was shocked the first time she heard this style on *NPR*. She said:

I thought, 'Oh my god, how can this person be talking like this on the radio?' Then I played it for my students, and I said, 'How does she sound?' and they said, 'Good, authoritative.' And that was when I knew that I had a problem...That I was not a part of the generation that understood what that style means...There's been a change and those of us who are bothered by some of these features are probably just getting old.

So I wasn't bothered or even the slightest bit annoyed by the linguistic style of *Skimm This*, which has since 2023 stopped airing new episodes I'm not embarrassed to admit that I enjoyed the way the hosts sounded with their upward inflection and occasional Valspeak. In fact, it's one of the things I liked most about the podcast. I didn't find it superficial or see it as a sign of being less serious. In fact, for me that was part of the appeal.

I'm not saying I want to sound like the podcast's hosts or

---

39. Wolf, Naomi. "Young women, give up the vocal fry and reclaim your strong female voice." *The Guardian*, 24 July 2015, theguardian.com/commentisfree/2015/jul/24/vocal-fry-strong-female-voice

40. Gross, Terry, host. "From Upspeak To Vocal Fry: Are We 'Policing' Young Women's Voices?" *Fresh Air*, 23 July 2015, npr.org/2015/07/23/425608745/from-upspeak-to-vocal-fry-are-we-policing-young-womens-voices?t=1660897776956

millennials in general. I don't need to add these mannerisms to my own style of speaking. I don't want to speak fast when I have only just finally mastered speaking slowly. Plus, I already have a New York accent that I need to keep under control if I want to be understood outside of the tri-state area. But I'm not sure I would have listened to the podcast if it was hosted by someone with a more serious voice, think *A&E's* Elizabeth Vargas or the *BBC's* Mishal Husain. I just wouldn't have needed to listen to it, it would defeat the purpose of my listening. I listened to *Skimm This* because it made me feel like I was part of the millennial world. I was in the know, just like them, and that made me more youthful. Moreover, I got to keep studying millennials. I learned how they think and how they felt. I learned what's important and interesting to them, and what they thought was funny and not so funny. The fact is that there are 71 million millennials in the United States alone,[41] and they are a generation still filled with promise. I find promise to be exciting, it's about the future. I see the maturish daughter, wife, and mother that I have become but I still want to have a little bit of promise. So why not go further? Why not connect with Generation Z, the cohort after millennials? They are even younger, born from 1997 onward.[42] Well, I would feel ridiculous trying to relate to them, the space is just too wide between us. I think if I tried, it might have the opposite effect and make me feel older than I actually am. I don't want or need that.

How did I learn about *Skimm This*? I'm not a millennial. I wasn't born between 1981 and 1996 (but I only just missed out).[43] I didn't watch *The Parent Trap* starring actress Lindsay Lohan at sleepovers. I

---

41. "Millennials overtake Baby Boomers as America's largest generation." *Pew Research Center,* 28 April 2020,pewresearch.org/fact-tank/2020/04/28/millennials-overtake-baby-boomers-as-americas-largest-generation/

42. "Defining generations: Where Millennials end and Generation Z begins." *Pew Research Center,* 17 Jan. 2019,pewresearch.org/fact-tank/2019/01/17/where-millennials-end-and-generation-z-begins/

43. Defining generations: Where Millennials end and Generation Z begins." *Pew Research Center,* 17 Jan. 2019,pewresearch.org/fact-tank/2019/01/17/where-millennials-end-and-generation-z-begins/

grew up with the 1961 version of the film featuring Hayley Mills, and my mother didn't allow me or any of her other kids to participate in sleepovers. I'm not selfie crazed. I'm not the person falling off a cliff trying to get that great shot. (I don't go near cliffs.) I like the television show *Seinfeld*; the 1995 episode featuring the "The Soup Nazi" is my favorite. I loved the chef who wanted military-like discipline in his soup shop. He wanted silence, order in the line, and refused to sell soup to anyone who complained. His rules, Seinfeld's joke. Some millennials found what they saw as a parody of WWII concentration camps offensive; not for me, so I guess I'm a millennial light.

    I first heard about the media company theSkimm from one of my female (millennial-aged) study abroad students in Rome. It was the Fall 2013 semester, the first day of class on a warm summer day in late August, and I was explaining the basics of how things would work during the semester. I pointed out that to write about the news they needed to know what was going on in the world and therefore each week they would take a news quiz — 10 questions about the week's biggest stories. I instructed them to look at the home pages of some of the larger news organizations, the *BBC, CNN, BuzzFeed* and *HuffPost*. Then Jennifer from California asked, "Professor. Can I use theSkimm email like a news source?" I said, "What's theSkimm?" And she said with uptalk, "It's this email I get every morning and it literally gives me the news in a really cool way." I said, "okay, why not, as long as it covers the biggest stories." I then wrote down "theSkimm," with the words "take a look!" on my notepad.

    Later I went to theSkimm's website. The startup was founded in 2012 by two women — Danielle Weisberg and Carly Zakin — who wanted to help millennials get informed and "become smarter." The duo, who coincidentally first met while studying abroad in Rome, came up with the idea on their sofa while they worked as news producers for *NBC*. Since 2012 they have raised nearly $30 million in funding[44] mostly from female investors, including American television producer Shonda Rhimes, television personality and model

---

44. Gross, Elana Lyn. "TheSkimm Is Launching A Daily News Podcast." *Forbes*, 25 Feb. 2019. forbes.com/sites/deloitte/2022/07/15/greening-aviation-reducing-emissions-along-the-aircraft-value-chain/?sh=714c2328b044

Tyra Banks, and Dean of USC Annenberg School for Communication and Journalism Willow Bay. I thought I should subscribe, especially if this was how some of my students were accessing news. I wanted to know what issues were important to them, but more importantly what approach and format they used to access news. This way, I could better understand how their minds worked. I signed up (using a second email address, the one I use for personal communications, not for business or work). I started receiving the emails each day. The headlines were snappy and catchy — "It Ain't Easy Being Independent"[45] about Catalonia's deadline to declare its independence from Spain and "Russian Into The DMs" about[46] Congress calling technology companies to testify about Russian interference in the U.S. election. The writing style is very conversational, lots of "yeahs"[47] but informative and with enough context to understand the story, especially if you know nothing about the issue.

The newsletter, though, certainly wasn't a model for journalism or old school journalism studies. It didn't adhere to any professional writing style, and this I found irritating. I wanted to print it out, edit, clean it up a bit. I know, the printing it out part sounds geriatric. Sorry about that. Like I said, millennial light. The writers used slang like "that'll show'em"[48] or "what the eff is going on."[49] They wrote

---

45. TheSkimm. "It Ain't Easy Being Independent." *TheSkimm Newsletter*, 16 Oct. 2017, Web. theskimm.com/archive/2017-10-16

46. TheSkimm. "Russian into the DMs." TheSkimm Newsletter, 2 Nov. 2017, Web. theskimm.com/archive/2017-11-02

47. TheSkimm. "Decision Made." *TheSkimm Newsletter*, 21 Nov. 2018, Web. theskimm.com/archive/2018-11-21

48. TheSkimm. "Mayday." *TheSkimm Newslette*r, 15 March 2018, Web. ttheskimm.com/archive/2018-03-15

49. TheSkimm. "Trump's Russia Connections: People to know." *TheSkimm Newsletter*, 21 Aug. 2017, Web.

50. TheSkimm. "Decision Made." *TheSkimm Newsletter*, 21 Nov. 2018, Web. theskimm.com/archive/2018-11-21

"Exclamation Point"[50] instead of using the symbol. And the thing that made me crazy were the extra letters they added to words to emphasize them, such as when they talked about the Federal Reserve chairman position and said, "which means the Fed chair is kiiiind of a big deal."[51] So for me, the style which works so well in a spoken-word podcast is a nightmare in written form. I hate when words are spelled incorrectly. In spite of the style, I didn't unsubscribe to the newsletter and instead it became an email that I quickly scanned over each day. Like me, thousands and thousands of people signed up, and the last time I checked there were seven million subscribers.[52]

However, with the newsletter's reach came a lot of pushback and criticism from more sophisticated media organizations. In the *WNYC* podcast *Note to Self*, host Manoush Zomorodi[53] said she was concerned about the "dumbing down" that embodies theSkimm's newsletter and that the content was not thorough enough to completely understand the issues. And while Zomorodi was delicate with her commentary, Christina Cauterucci in the online magazine *Slate*[54] was aggressive. She compared theSkimm's format of pairing serious news with conversational quips to a high-school history teacher rapping about current events. "Imagine if Politico's Playbook were translated by a chatbot that learned the English language from *The Simple Life*, *Daily Mail* headlines, and *Nick Jr.*," she wrote. Moreover, she said the newsletter was insulting to its target audience — young women. The readers are treated as if they've never read an article, looked at a map, or accidentally seen a *CNN* segment in their

---

51. TheSkimm. "Russian into the DMs." *TheSkimm Newsletter*, 2 Nov. 2017, Web. theskimm.com/archive/2017-11-02

52. Malone, Noreen. "The Skimm Brains 7 million people wake up to their newsletter, and their voice, every morning." *The Cut,* Vox Media, 28 Oct. 2018

53. Zomorodi, Manoush, host. "What Happens when we Skimm the News." *Note to Self,* WNYC Studios. 15 June 2016, wnycstudios.org/podcasts/notetoself/episodes/skimm-news-millennial

54. Cauterucci, Christina. "The Skimm Is the Ivanka Trump of Newsletters." *Slate,* 17 May 2017. slate.com/human-interest/2017/05/the-skimm-a-chic-news-digest-for-women-is-the-newsletter-version-of-ivanka-trump.html

dentists' waiting rooms. Its patronizing tone assumes that female news consumers tune out anything of importance if it's not processed through verbal eyerolls.

The criticism didn't stop theSkimm. They continued to do what they did and much more. For years I was bombarded with promotional emails about their other media products — smartphone app, bestselling book, and lots of events. Not for me, thanks. But the podcasts were a different matter. I began with *9 to 5ish with theSkimm* (first called *Skimm'd from the Couch*), a weekly podcast they launched in February 2018 where women talk about their path to success. Thank God, this is still around. Then in 2019 they started to build momentum with *Skimm This*, and it was exactly what I needed something young and hip while I was getting older in Germany. I wasn't preoccupied about editing the script because it wasn't in front of me like the newsletter. I took it all in, and it was refreshing and transportive. I also started buying face creams with three hyaluronic acids. Like the song goes, "Keep young and beautiful. If you want to be loved."

XOXO podcasts

I talk about podcasts with love, *amore*, and *Liebe*. I know that podcasts have helped me to survive living in Germany thanks to my support network of hosts helping and guiding me day in and day out. I have calmed my fears and concerns when it comes to raising my kids and taking care of my body. I have an on-demand tutor for my prayer practice. I have opportunities to escape and laugh hard when I need it most. I have news and information that keeps me informed about what's going on in the world and what's happening back in New York.

I guess the question is why podcasts? Why not social media or television or even radio, which I have always liked. Why are podcasts occupying such an important, all-encompassing role in my life now? There are so many reasons why these audio files that are freely distributed over the internet are now my preferred media choice and most of it has to do with flexibility and choice.

Let me explain a bit how podcasting came to be. The actual practice of using the internet to make digital audio files available for downloading to a computer or mobile device began as an idea at a meeting in 2000 between David Winer, a software engineer and weblogger, and Adam Curry, best known his role as a former MTV video jockey (and his mullet hairstyle). They wanted to provide delivery and automatic synchronization for audio and video content so that people (like me) were not stuck sitting at a computer in order to enjoy a show.[55] It took some time, but they played with the software enough until they learned how to syndicate MP3 files online.

---

55. Cochrane, Todd. *Podcasting: The Do-It-Yourself Guide*. Wiley Publishing, Indiana. 2005. Print.

I told you already, I'm so grateful to these guys.

They talked up the media form as revolutionary and they were right because it opened up communication in a different way. Podcasting, a term invented in 2004 by Ben Hammersley in a blog post in *The Guardian*,[56] allowed hosts to have a conversation with their listeners, they weren't like radio reporters and producers worried about regulation and pressure from management. They could, with inexpensive, even free, technology, share their ideas and beliefs about any topic (especially the ones that mainstream media wasn't covering) while also developing an audience and it was amazing.

Think about it, in 2005 Nick van der Kolk could now tell experimental stories, the ones that didn't fit into the radio story mould, on his podcast called *Love + Radio*. In 2009, Comedian Marc Maron got really personal in his 90-minute interview driven podcast called *WTF*, which stems from the internet slang initialism for the expression "What the fuck?." We all know it's nearly impossible for users to stay engaged on any social media platform for that long. The podcast's success — it averages five million downloads per month[57] — showed the digital media's ability to attract and keep a loyal, subscriber-based audience. Later came the 2014 true crime podcast *Serial* that reinvestigated the case of Adnan Syed, who was convicted of first-degree murder for the 1999 killing of Hae Min Lee, a high school senior and Syed's classmate. The podcast that raised questions about the conviction and his legal representation was the first to hit five million downloads on Apple's iTunes[58] and brought podcasting into the mainstream.

This was all coupled with Apple giving podcasting an endorsement, sort of like a giant thumbs up, when in 2005 it created

---

56. Hammersley, Ben. "Audible Revolution." *The Guardian*. 12 Feb. 2004. Web. Accessed 25 Feb. 2018.

57. Ullrich, Jeff, host. "Brendan McDonald, WTF Producer." *The Wolf Den*. EarWolf. Episode 55. 10 April 2014. earwolf.com/episode/brendan-mcdonald-wtf-producer/

58. Dredge, Stuart. "Serial podcast breaks iTunes records as it passes 5m downloads and streams." *The Guardian*. 18 November 2014. Web. Accessed 18 May 2017.

a podcast directory inside the iTunes stores that allowed people to discover, subscribe, manage, and freely listen to podcasts. And then later in 2015 it created its first standalone Podcasts app. And since then, there are podcast only networks, which manage a group of shows and provide them with marketing and advertising help, and the mainstream media has expanded its footprint into the business recognizing podcasting's opportunity for news, information, and of course storytelling. The fact is that podcasting is now a standard part of digital media today. I actually prefer podcasts from the so-called professional output not only because of the quality but also the source credibility. I feel like I can trust what I am hearing, but hey that's me. I'm old school that way.

For me the on-demand personalization is what fits my lifestyle. I can curate my listening because that podcast app on my phone is like my own personal library, and everything is available — woohoo! I mostly help myself to American podcasts, a few British, and even some in Italian. I pick and choose what I want and again that control factor for someone like me is quite thrilling. I also like the all-mine intimacy, nobody-knows what-I'm-listening to part. If I don't like what I'm hearing or the podcast host or even guests say something that upsets me or pisses me off, then I can stop listening or even delete the show. I don't have to get into the details or explain to my husband why I am changing the channel or turning off the radio. I can do whatever I want.

I also know that my extensive podcast listening has to do with technology. The emerging and evolving technologies that support voice, like smartphones, smart speakers with voice assistants, connected cars, along with broadband access created new and super easy ways for me and millions of other users to listen to podcasts. I am a pretty consistent person and so I mostly listen on my phone, but I sometimes use my smart speaker (which I unplug each night because I know companies are spying on me) and also listen a lot in my car. I even make my kids listen to storytelling podcasts during long car rides. I download them when I can. I am not tied to a screen. I don't always need an internet connection to engage. I listen when I have time.

I appreciate the choice because it makes me feel in control and also because these options fit in well with my chronically interrupted life. Like you already know, I have young kids and they always seem to desperately need something. They also have a lot of questions. I swear it feels like together they ask me at least 100 questions a day. I know they are trying to make sense of the world. And while they do try to be polite when they say, "Excuse me, Mommy," they still interrupt me all the time. I constantly have to stop whatever I'm doing and try to answer questions like: Why does your shadow follow you? Who would win in a fight between daddy and a killer whale? Do dinosaurs live in Germany? If I'm listening to podcasts, it's easy because I pause for however long I need, which could be a few seconds, several minutes, even hours, and then I easily pick up where I left off on any one of my devices. Do you understand now why I'm all XOXO with podcasts?

Catholic fidem

For more than five years, I worked for the Holy See, the Vatican. The job was interesting, exciting, and even prestigious too. It was also very stressful; the Vatican's communications output is always highly scrutinized. I had to be very careful with the words I used to communicate any message or idea. I had to be at the top of my game, all the time, every day.

I worked in the Palazzo Maffei Marescotti on Via della Pigna, just down the block from the Pantheon, in the historic center of Rome. The thick, white line around the building marked entry into Vatican territory. The *palazzo* is beautiful with a grand courtyard and a fountain. Inside, the organized office space is filled with religious symbols — a crucifix in every room, statues of the Blessed Mother, and paintings depicting scenes from the Bible. Like every company or organization, there was a workplace culture, and this one was based on the beliefs and hierarchy of the Roman Catholic Church.

The people I directly responded to were priests, monsignors, and cardinals. There was protocol to follow. It was never "Excuse me, Joe," but instead was "Excuse me, Your Excellency," and "Excuse me, Most Reverend Eminence." I had to learn these titles and use them appropriately. I already had to be careful with my Italian, especially my usage of the formal and informal forms of you, such as *tu, voi, lei,* and *loro*. In English, there is only one way to say you — you! There was also an unofficial dress code. The Vatican was definitely not the place for self-expression or high style. I was young and what I thought was hip at the time. I loved clothes, I was in Italy, known for its meticulous craftsmanship and luxury materials, but in the Vatican I needed simple skirts and pants, nothing that would draw attention to me or God forbid a second glance. I started to look more and more nun-like. I kept a large, Virgin Mary blue shawl in my desk that I would put on if I was called into a meeting and happened to be wearing a cap or no sleeve dress or shirt. I could never enter a room full of priests with my arms uncovered. I did it once and it was horrible — I felt so exposed, so naked. I even had to think about my feet. The day I wore black, open toe heels I was pulled aside by an older female colleague who told me they were an absolute "no-no," because toes were not to be seen, even in the Roman summer heat. I thought this was extreme: what about the Franciscan friars who wear those Birkenstock-like sandals? I compromised. I kept wearing sandals, but I toned down my nail polish colors — no bright reds, no blue or purples anymore, just barely there, baby pink.

The greatest thing about the job was not the interesting work, definitely not the written and unwritten rules, and not even the private health insurance or the tax-free shopping at the supermarket and high-end retail store (which I must admit were pretty fantastic). For me, it was the religious opportunities. If I wanted, I could participate in daily mass. I could be confessed by one of the priests in our office. If I was struggling with something, I could take my pick of religious and lay people for advice. I had a whole community of religious support in Italy. I was encouraged to attend spiritual retreats for Advent and Lent, as well conferences for other religious holidays, which were wonderful learning experiences. I even participated in a number of pilgrimages including visiting Lourdes, Fátima in Portugal and Santiago de Compostela. I was especially moved by the pilgrimage in the footsteps of St. Paul in Syria (before it was a dangerous war zone), as well as the papal journey to the Holy Land in 2009 with Pope Benedict XVI. I was not only working but I was learning about my faith. I was beginning to love and appreciate it more. I was building my relationship with God and felt I was getting closer to him. I also appreciated the sensation that I was part of a big project. When I left my job after my daughter was born, I started to miss those moments of prayer, reflection, and spiritual conviviality. I needed faith, more than ever in Germany. I wanted to feel less scared about things. I also needed guidance and strength to help me through this period peacefully in the very heartland of the Reformation.

I have always struggled to pray and meditate on my own. I can't just pick up the Bible, read a passage, tilt my head to the side, reflect, and then have an "oh, interesting" moment. I'm too easily distracted when I pray. I think about things that have absolutely nothing to do with prayer — "Are the kids' school clothes ready for tomorrow?" "Do I want those shoes from Zalando?" God, please forgive me for being so unfocused. I'm often interrupted by my kids, my husband, and the news alerts and notifications on my phone. I turn my cell to silent mode, but I can still hear the buzzing. I should probably leave it in another room. In church, I'm a bit all over the place. I have always attended mass regularly and while I did often get caught up in my own spiraling thoughts, I was always able to pick up a little something valuable or thought provoking from the hour-long celebration. But now with my kids, as you can surely imagine, I'm almost exclusively focused on their behavior, and I can hardly follow the mass. I threaten my daughter with "stop, or you're going to time-out when we go home" and it works now that she's a bit older, but my son is still a handful. I struggle to get him to sit, to be quiet. I work hard to shush and distract him with toys and food. I just pray that the mass moves along quickly, that my son doesn't choke, and we manage not to attract too much attention. I imagine the other super moms laughing and saying with disdain, "Look —she only has two and can't control them."

All this is why I needed to get some type of guided spirituality back in my life and my blessed podcasts were able to fill this void for me. I wasn't interested in Catholic comedy or pop culture like what *The Jen Fulwiler Show* podcast offers, even though host/comedian Jennifer Fulwiler is funny. I didn't want interviews with high-profile personalities who discussed how faith influenced their lives like the *Journeys of Faith with Paula Faris* podcast. I found it too newsy for this area of my listening. I also didn't want a podcast that gave me a somewhat theatrical feeling like the *Letters from Home* podcast from the St. Paul Center for Biblical Theology. The episodes are often short reflections, but they sound too much like radio evangelism, which I really dislike. I needed a podcast that I could use to pray and meditate. I wanted a podcast that could help answer some questions about my Catholic faith and deepen it. I also wanted a podcast that would help me engage with some of the big issues. I needed podcasts that could minister, preach, and teach me things.

I tried several mediation-prayer podcasts before finding the right one for me. I listened to many episodes of the top ranked *Daily Meditation Podcast,* a secular show hosted by Mary Meckley, but the episodes felt more like therapy and self-help with its "you're wonderful" and "you're safe" type of comments. That wasn't the kind of support I needed. I also listen to the *Pray As You Go,* a daily podcast from the Jesuit Media Initiatives in Britain. The Jesuits are a religious order founded by Ignatius of Loyola during the Counter Reformation who see education as a path to a meaningful life of leadership and service. Pope Francis is a Jesuit. The episodes are well produced, with beautiful music, just like the reviews said they would be. I try to listen regularly at night when I'm in bed. I'm comfortable there, head on my pillow, lying face up. I find the daily episodes to be a peaceful, yet guided, way to unwind after a full day. The episodes are short, only about ten minutes long, and use the Church's daily readings as the starting point. The reflection ends with something comforting like talk to Jesus about how you would like him to be more present in your own life or what might Jesus be promising you, speak to him about what you see or what you would like him to see. The episodes end with the Glory Be prayer. I'm so relaxed when I listen that I sometimes fall asleep. I don't think that's the point, but I figure it's okay.

I thought it would be great to listen with Marco. I like the saying "the couple that prays together stays together" but it's not something he wants to do. He comes to mass with me and the kids, that's his thing. I thought that since the episodes were short, I could convince him to take a break from one of the self-defense YouTube channels that he watches almost every night in bed. He is always ready for a fight. He did reluctantly listen with me one night and when it was over I happily asked, "Isn't it great, right?" He said, "No, I don't like it." Now I listen in bed with headphones. But I do, sometimes, find them on his nightstand in the morning.

I can also meditate with *The Pope's Voice* podcast by Vatican Radio, which allows me to hear Pope Francis' public speeches, most of which are in Italian. The episodes include the Holy Father's Angelus prayers (Sundays) and his General Audience speech (Wednesdays). I was lucky because when I worked at the Vatican I participated in these events on several occasions. I went to the General Audience once with Chris Gardner, whose life story was the basis for the Hollywood film *The Pursuit of Happyness* starring Will Smith in 2006. The thing is that these are not one-to-two or one-to-20 events, there are many other people. They don't just sit or stand and listen, they muscle around for a better view, they take a lot of photos, and there is always the occasional person who attempts to rush the stage and touch the Pope. But at home in GK the podcast brings the Holy Father to me personally. I can hear his grandfatherly voice in Italian. I also like to hear him speak a few words in English as well. This is such a powerful listening experience, and for me it's the podcast that proved beyond doubt all the industry claims about podcasting's intimacy. Thanks to earbuds the voices and the words from these podcasts "roost there, rubbing shoulders with your own thoughts."[59]

For short conversational reflections about everything from prayer to faith to tattoos and transgenderism, I listen to *The Fr. Mike Schmitz Podcast*. Produced by Ascension Press, the podcast evolved from Fr. Schmitz's self-titled YouTube series. Fr. Schmitz is the director of the Office of Youth Ministry for the Diocese of Duluth, Minnesota and the chaplain for the University of Minnesota-Duluth's Newman Center. He sounds young and charismatic and talks fast. His down-to-earth tone makes me feel as if I'm listening to a friend, and like a real friend or family member he doesn't always say what I want to hear. The episode "Is Swearing a Sin?,"[60] didn't ease my Catholic guilt about my occasional use of curse words. I only swear when I'm worked up about something, and I don't do it in front of my kids. I control myself and say "oh, snap," "holy cannoli," "f-no" if they are around. I felt better about my occasional use of swearing after I learned from a study that people who swear have a bigger vocabulary

---

[59]. Weldon, Glen, host. "It's All In Your Head: The One-Way Intimacy Of Podcast Listening." *Pop Culture Happy Hour*, NPR, 2 Feb. 2018, npr.org/2018/02/02/582105045/its-all-in-your-head-the-one-way-intimacy-of-podcast-listening

[60]. Schmitz, Fr. Mike, host. "Is Swearing a Sin?" *The Fr. Mike Schmitz Catholic Podcast*, Ascension Press, 23 Jan. 2020, media.ascensionpress.com/podcast/is-swearing-a-sin/

and are more fluent when it comes to language.[61] Moreover, the study noted that curse words are a way to express strong emotion and are not emblematic of people who have no self-control.

So, I was hoping Fr. Schmitz was going to agree and say something like, "No, it's not a problem. God is not worried about this kind of petty stuff, there are big sins out there in the world like murder." But he didn't, and I said "Oh, shit," again. In the about seven-minute episode Fr. Schmitz laid out the three times when curse words can be sinful: 1. If you use a vulgar word against someone. I have done that. 2. If you use a word connected to a sexual act because sex between persons is meant to be holy. I have done that too. 3. If you use a vulgar word in public because it could scandalize people. I don't do that. The point, he said, "words matter" and the words that people use reflect what's in their heart. I thought, "how awful, I don't want these f-ing words in my heart." I try not to curse, but it's not easy.

I was also immediately interested in the episode "Why Is Prayer So Hard?"[62] because I have asked myself this question a lot. I already mentioned that I'm often distracted when I pray and my mind wanders. I feel terrible about it, I do. I want to be more disciplined in my prayer practice. Fr. Schmitz called it right out and said, "prayer is a battle" that we fight against ourselves. He went personal and said he often comes up with a thousand other things he could possibly do instead of praying. He said he has to sometimes fight to get himself to pray. He said it takes a big effort to be truly present during prayer. So how do I win this tough battle? I thought Fr. Schmitz would talk about a special method or technique that I could use, a good sound way to tackle this problem. But instead, he explained that if I wanted to improve my prayer practice then I needed to set aside a space for faith. He said I should make the intentional, on purpose, and faithful

---

61. Swanson, Ana. "Why it's a good sign if you curse a lot." *The Washington Post*, 22 Dec. 2015, washingtonpost.com/news/wonk/wp/2015/12/22/why-its-a-good-sign-if-you-curse-a-lot/

62. Schmitz, Fr. Mike, host. "Why is Prayer so Hard?" *The Fr. Mike Schmitz Catholic Podcast*, Ascension Press, 14 Nov. 2019, media.ascensionpress.com/podcast/why-is-prayer-so-hard/

decision to live outside of prayer the way I want to live inside prayer. I needed to include the virtues of prayer throughout my distracted, often worry-filled day. This sounded hard, really hard. On his advice, I ask God for what I need, out loud (if no one is around) even if it might be embarrassing or selfish. For example: I want a career again. I want my hair to be healthier. I wouldn't mind having a cool friend to hang out with occasionally. At least now, I'm talking to God.

When I listened to the episode "How to Live this Lent for Others"[63] I realized that my Easter preparation these past few years was completely wrong and self-centered. I grew up in the States with this notion that something had to be given up for Lent. I found more of the same in Italy. I have always been somewhat proud of myself for being strong and successfully fasting from things I enjoyed. I found it to be a personal challenge. I love challenges. I always sacrificed food, but more than just meat on Fridays during Lent. I gave up pasta one year, 40 days without pasta was hard, and another year, I gave up peanut butter, which I spread on hot toast most mornings. I didn't know anything about the local German Lenten traditions because I frequented Sunday mass on the GK Base, and the priest is an American captain in the Air Force. He does Lent the American way. I did learn that this region, North Rhine-Westphalia, of Germany was heavily into *Karneval*, which marked the last period of drinking and so-called fun before Lent. They were also serious about Good Friday, known as *Karfreitag*, because it was a national holiday, unlike in Catholic Italy or the United States, where there are fewer such holidays.

Fr. Schmitz said Lent is more than digging in and being disciplined. He noted that discipline is a great virtue, but it's personal and "all about me." He said there is another step that Catholics can take during Lent and that's to be generous, which expands our hearts and deepens our relationship with others. He said to move away from discipline and ask God, "What do you want from me?" The answer could be many things, including helping others in need, donating to

---

63. Schmitz, Fr. Mike, host. "How to Live this Lent for Others" *The Fr. Mike Schmitz Catholic Podcast,* Ascension Press, 27 Feb. 2020, media.ascensionpress.com/podcast/how-to-live-this-lent-for-others/

charity, or praying more, which all require discipline but also generosity.

For insight into big Catholic issues, I turned to *The Catholic Feminist* podcast. To my disappointment the show stopped releasing new episodes in 2020. Host Claire Swinarski talked to different women each week who use their gifts to build up the Church. She started each episode with the same question: What does your life as a Catholic feminist look like? I have never described myself as a feminist but that didn't matter.

Swinarski, who is from Milwaukee, sounded like the sweetest thing with her "hey y'all" opening. She reminded me of my young millennial friends at the *Skimm This* podcast, but her vocabulary includes a lot of "God," not the exclamative "Oh God!" the real one, "Lord," and "Body of Christ." The podcast's audio was a bit raw; it sounded like she recorded the podcast from somewhere in her home with simple technology. There is no studio and major editing here but that didn't stop Swinarski from talking about big issues, like postpartum depression, pornography, human trafficking, immigration, and racism. She was also not afraid to say when the Church made mistakes, which I appreciated and respected, but sometimes I wished she would have been a bit more forthright. The episodes are long, at least 40 minutes each, and I often listened to this podcast when I had big chunks of time like when I was waiting for my daughter to finish one of her extracurricular activities. I probably should have tried to socialize with the other parents but that felt too awkward and hard. I'm a cat that walks by herself. I just put my earbuds in and acted like I was busy.

I was listening to *The Catholic Feminist* while waiting for my daughter at a ballet lesson when I felt my heart pounding. It was an episode about being a special needs mother.[64] I listened as Swinarski asked Vania Deeney, a Catholic from Minnesota, to share her story about being a special needs mom. Deeney said she had an uneventful pregnancy until her third trimester when she was told that her unborn

---

64. Swinarski, Claire, host. "Thriving as a Special Needs Parent ft. Vania Deeney." *The Catholic Feminist*, Episode 136, 19 Feb. 2020, thecatholicfeminist.com/shownotes/vania

baby had a series of birth anomalies. The information was "shocking" and "totally rocked our world," she said. Her daughter was born with one eye and a blockage in her intestines. She was later diagnosed with SOX2 syndrome, a rare disorder characterized by abnormal development of the eyes and other body parts. Deeney added that most parents don't imagine having a child who needs a lot of extra help and attention and it's scary and isolating, especially since many people are afraid to interact with someone who is different. Asked if she ever felt resentful or upset with God, Deeney said she struggled with the "why me?" and "why us?" for some time. She said, though, ultimately that her daughter's diagnosis has strengthened her faith, challenged her to lean into God more, and reminded her that her daughter is God's child. "I just have the privilege of being her caretaker on earth," Deeney said.

The episode brought back memories of when I was pregnant with my daughter and like I already said after an ultrasound at about five months, my husband and I were told there could be a genetic malformation. I sat in the doctor's office in Rome thinking that I had misunderstood what they said in Italian, that I had gotten the translation wrong in my head but that was not the case. I had an immediate, what was considered late term, amniocentesis. I was afraid, scared of what they would find, what they would tell me. I remember my husband rushing in and out of the bathroom while I waited to undergo the exam. I prayed. I turned to God, to the Blessed Mother. I prayed to Our Lady of Childbirth. I visited the Church of St. Augustine in Rome, where there was a statue of her by Jacopo Sansovino from 1521, which meant a lot to me. The result came back negative. I was thankful but I didn't find any peace until my daughter was born and the doctors told me she was whole and healthy. Her Apgar score,[65] a 10, was the highest possible.

I don't for a moment believe that because I prayed or believed in God more than Deeney somehow I was blessed. I don't believe faith relieves suffering. In fact, I think it redeems it. I thought about how

---

65. "Apgar Score." *U.S. Centers for Disease Control and Prevention*, 6 Aug. 2019, cdc.gov/nchs/nvss/facility-worksheets-guide/32.htm?Sort=URL%3A%3Aasc&Categories=Newborn%20Information

fortunate I was, how fortunate I am, how grateful I am. I forget sometimes. I get wrapped up in other stuff. I should know better. By the time the episode wrapped up, I could see the other parents start to move towards the ballet studio to pick up their kids. I took out my earbuds and picked up my daughter. I hugged her super tight, and she said, "Ouch, mommy, you're hurting me." I didn't care.

Another episode of the podcast brought the abortion debate to the table, but through a side door.[66] It was moving but it also left me upset. Swinarski spoke to Martha Farnsworth, an adoptee and birth mom from Idaho, about her unplanned pregnancy at 18 years old and her decision to give up her daughter for adoption. Swinarski explained that many view adoption as a "healthy, beautiful choice," but it also includes loss and darkness and it's difficult, maybe even more difficult than abortion. I honestly never thought about adoption this way. I'm not part of the pro-life movement. I'm not out there protesting abortion. But I can see the argument that adoption may be a good choice in some cases. I don't like the way the issue has become so divisive in the USA. I don't think abortion is a good thing, but I do think there are circumstances when it can be justified. I know Church doctrine says otherwise but I disagree. And I don't think God is upset with me because I feel this way.

Through tears, Farnsworth said she struggled emotionally with the grief and pain of carrying her baby for nine months and later having to say goodbye. She has an open adoption, which means she has a relationship with her birth daughter and her adoptive parents, which includes annual visits. Farnsworth said her local Catholic church and community weren't understanding or sympathetic. "I wish I could say that my church was the place that I felt comfortable going to for support, but it wasn't," she said. The community was focused on her out of wedlock pregnancy. Because of this scrutiny she drove 30 minutes to another church on Sundays. I wished Swinarski would have called out the judgmental behavior of Farnsworth's parish more directly. I wanted her to be like "what, the f***", this is bull s***,"

---

66. Swinarski, Claire, host. "The Sacrifice of Being a Birth Mother" *The Catholic Feminist*, Episode 137, 26 Feb. 2020, thecatholicfeminist.com/shownotes/martha

okay, no curse words, but I wanted clear cut disapproval. Instead, she said, "I just think about how devastated that must have made Jesus. I don't think your situation was super pleasing to him."

For me, healthy faith asks questions and holds all people accountable. I feel that questioning needs to happen more. Not just from secular critics but from the inside, from the people who have faith, the supporters, those that actually believe, care, and love the Church. I was upset by how the cases of child sexual abuse in the United States were handled. I'm concerned about conservative traditionalists who are at odds with Pope Francis. I don't understand how some Church leaders could be so out of touch with first world feminist language. I think it's eye opening and funny that the Barbie Savior Instagram account[67] parodies volunteer selfies in Africa where many Catholics go on mission trips. The fact is these things, including how Farnsworth's community responded to her pregnancy, don't rock my faith or make me want to become an atheist. They just confirm for me that there are a lot of stupid Catholics out there, just as there are a lot of stupid people of other creeds or those with no belief.

I learned about the importance of letting go in *The Catholic Feminist* episode with Jeannie Gaffigan.[68] Swinarski spoke to Gaffigan about her book *When Life Gives You Pears: The Healing Power of Faith, Family and Funny People* and more specifically how she handled the diagnosis of a brain tumor in 2017. Gaffigan is married to comedian Jim Gaffigan, and their family is known for being Catholic and numerous, with five kids. She's a writer and was also executive producer of her husband's self-titled television show. She said her diagnosis was like "the story of when St. Paul got knocked off his horse on the road." The story is that Paul fell in amazement from his horse when Christ appeared to him amid a blinding light. I know this one — during my pilgrimage in Syria, I visited St. Paul's conversion site in Damascus. I

---

67. Barbie Savior [@barbiesavior] "I know I am supposed to be resting…"

68. Swinarski, Claire, host. "Letting go of Our Addiction to Control ft. Jeannie Gaffigan." *The Catholic Feminist*, Episode 125, 2 Oct. 2019, thecatholicfeminist.com/shownotes/jeannie

even took a picture at the site. Gaffigan said that after her diagnosis she had let go and stopped being the "executive producer" of her family. Yes, emails went unanswered, the to-do list remained long, but the world kept going on and everything was fine. She said her husband grew as a caregiver and her kids became more responsible, but control is still an issue. Note to self. Listen to this woman! Gaffigan said her faith helped her through this challenging time. I haven't been given terrible health news, thank you God, and I wouldn't think about comparing myself to Gaffigan or her situation, but I too as you know have lots of inner turbulence and I'm dependent on my faith and podcasts to get me through.

That crappy feeling

I feel like crap sometimes. I feel tired and stressed from all the worrying. I feel bloated and full no matter what I eat. I feel especially guilty about being so far away from my family. I don't know exactly why I feel this way, but I don't like it.

I didn't have the kind of parents who laid the guilt trip on me about living overseas. I never heard them say "stay home" or "don't go;" and they weren't passive aggressive. I swear. I knew they missed me, and I missed them too. They were very different from my mother-in-law who complained that we lived far away — even when we lived in Rome and she was in Naples, just a two-and-a-half-hour drive — and that her three children, especially my husband, didn't love her enough. I tried hard to help my aging parents even though I was thousands of miles away. I called every day, often more than once. I oversaw their online banking. I made doctor's appointments. I ordered prescription refills. I also visited as much as possible, at least twice a year. I didn't organize vacations to new, never-before-visited places, I always went back to New York. I wanted to. Fortunately, Marco understood.

I started to feel more overwhelmed by my guilt when my father started to have debilitating health issues. I felt like a terrible daughter. I wanted to be there more for him, but also for my mother who was his caregiver at home. I continued to visit as much as I could but work and family responsibilities didn't always allow for more trips. I did spend a lot of time on the phone with my father. I did my best to comfort and advise him on his ailments with phrases like "it's normal for someone your age," "don't worry, things come and go," and "be calm, don't stress."

A few months before he passed away, I planned a last-minute visit to New York on Christmas Eve. Together with Marco and my daughter, I pulled into the driveway with our rented car, rang the doorbell, and surprised everyone. I felt like I was in my own version of a Folgers Coffee commercial, but instead of "Peter" coming home for Christmas it was me, their Rosey.

The holiday was nice because I was with my whole family, but also sad because my father wasn't well. Then three days later, he said he was having trouble breathing, my mother and I brushed it off thinking he was having a sort of anxiety attack, which had happened before. We even made him chamomile tea, not realizing that he had shortness of breath and his lips were white. But when Marco saw him, he said this was more than anxiety. I rode with him in the ambulance to the hospital as the sirens blared. It was like one of those medical television dramas. I was scared.

The prognosis wasn't good, my father had suffered a heart attack. He had a blockage, but we would later learn that he wasn't a candidate for a stent because he was too fragile. He was stable and after a few days he left the hospital for a rehabilitation center. "We just have to wait and see," the doctor said. That didn't seem right, or easy. I didn't know if I should stay or go back to Germany as planned, but my mother insisted I return to my home. "There is nothing you can do, if things change, we will let you know," she said.

Less than two months later, in February, my father relapsed. He suddenly stopped moving and was having trouble breathing. I needed to get back to New York immediately because they said there wasn't much time. The next morning, my daughter and I were on a flight out of Frankfurt. I was proud of how well-behaved she was on the flight as if she understood at three years old what was going to happen. I landed in the early afternoon and my older brother, brought me directly to the hospital. I saw and learned that my father was being kept alive by continuous positive airway pressure therapy, or CPAP, which the doctors politely told me feels like you're driving on the highway at 65 mph with your head out the window. I told him that I loved him and that he was a wonderful father. And through the mask, he told me in Italian *fatti forte*, which means "be strong." He also said that he was thirsty and wanted the awful mask off. I felt even worse knowing that he had to endure additional hours of CPAP for me. It is true that parents always try to put their children first, even on their deathbeds. The next morning all the tubes were removed, and he was comforted with morphine. Less than 24 hours later he passed away. I held his left hand, my mother his right, as he took his last breaths. It was calm, but terribly sad. I had to be there, not my older sister who had already done so much, I sent her home to watch our kids, or my older brothers, who were grown, strong men. I wanted it to be me.

In most Italian families, the daughter or daughters know that they will take care of their parents, and since I lived overseas my sister oversaw almost everything. I knew that my brothers basically just visited my parents, they were more involved with their wives' families, but still, I wasn't around as much so I should be the one there. It was my responsibility. I deserved the anguish that comes with seeing a parent in their last moments on earth. I often forget the exact date my father passed away, but I clearly remember his last moments. I can't forget them, even if I wanted to.

I talk about everything with my mother and sister, but my daughter guilt wasn't something I wanted to share with them or even Marco, who often bears the brunt of my complaints, worries, and ailments. The *Dear Sugars* podcast helped me to better understand my guilt and how to harness it. Hosted by Cheryl Strayed and Steve Almond, the show is a giant dose of empathy and encouragement. The episodes start with the hosts reading an anonymous letter from someone about some important, usually heart-wrenching topic. The two don't provide a quick-fix solution to the problem, but instead they talk about it and show how one person's struggle is often a universal one. This is the kind of podcast you listen to when you need a little perspective on your own obstacles, and I most definitely needed that. By the time I found *Dear Sugars*, a *WBUR* and *The New York Times* production, the project had already come to an end. The show, however, continues with re-releases of previously broadcasted episodes, and that's how I came across the episode about saying goodbye to our loved ones.[69]

---

69. Strayed, Cheryl and Steve Almond, hosts. "Saying Goodbye." *Dear Sugars*, WBUR and The New York Times, 16 Sept. 2016, wbur.org/dearsugar/2020/04/11/saying-goodbye

The episode was like putting a soothing ointment on my guilt, which is like a deep cut that I don't take much care of. I get along fine, but it's always there, sometimes I pick at it, and it bothers me. In the episode, a listener, called "daddy's girl," wrote about her father's Stage IV cancer diagnosis and her guilt about first studying and now living in another state some 17 hours away from her parents. She was happy but still felt as if she had abandoned them. She asked if she was being selfish. Strayed, who shared her own experience about her mother's death when she was 22 years old, said the most important thing to do was to "love the people you love with abandon and truth" and it's not "about being there every minute, but being present emotionally." Then she said, "you don't have to live in the same town as someone just because you love them dearly." Almond added that it's harder to be far away when a parent's illness is drawn out, it's more complicated, compared to when it's acute and sudden, it's therefore simplified. They encouraged "daddy's girl" to live her life, but also to be as involved as much as she could. Lastly, they said, just make sure you can do and say the things that are needed. I was able to at least do that with my father.

Another *Dear Sugars* episode that resonated with me was about finding a place, a location, that feels like home[70] and how many people struggle with this. I have worked hard in my about 15 years overseas to make every place I've lived feel like a real home, even if New York will always be home. I know that home is a metaphor for oneself. In this episode, Strayed and Almond talked to writer Pam Houston who gushed about the quality of light and the bigness of the sky of her "forever" home on a Colorado ranch. Well, I can't do that. I can't talk lovingly about the mostly gray, overcast, German sky. For me, the physical location, the address, the GPS coordinates, have to be secondary.

The inside, with all the material things, is what gives me happiness, contentment, love, and security and makes my home. For example, some of the paintings that hang on my walls were gifts from my

---

70. Strayed, Cheryl and Steve Almond, hosts. "Location, Location, Location." *Dear Sugars*, WBUR and The New York Times, 10 March 2017, wbur.org/dearsugar/2017/03/10/dear-sugar-episode-eighty-seven

parents. They were mostly picked by my father who loved art and they once adorned the walls of my childhood home. There are my mother's handmade runners and doilies that are lovingly located on various pieces of furniture. They are delicate and remind me of her. There are lots of photographs, especially ones of the important moments — weddings, baptisms, birthdays. There are various gifts from family and friends, like the dessert dishes I use on special occasions (from my friend Emily who I met as an undergraduate student at Hunter College) and the small 10-inch statue of the Virgin Mary holding a fruit basket that's in my kitchen (from my sister). There are my "Made in the USA" textiles. I only buy American sheets and towels — I swear by the cotton. I know, I might be attached to objects, I might be materialistic but these things in my home are positive emotional triggers that make me feel good if the outside world is making me feel bad.

In an article about the psychology of what's inside our homes,[71] Professor Samuel Gosling, author and psychotherapist Amy Morin, and executive therapeutic coach Lisa Pepper-Satkin explained that traces of our psyche are in our homes and the décor, including photographs, gifts, and memorabilia, become emblems of our experiences and therefore we attach deep value to them. These "things" tend to provoke a bunch of interesting emotions, and it's somewhat comforting to have them. I agree completely — look at me. I have surrounded myself with lots of familiar things in an unfamiliar place.

I keep all these "things" in a home that is super organized and clean. I've never slept in an unmade bed. I can't leave the house with an unmade bed; I would be obsessing over the chaos I left behind. I also don't want anyone, especially my kids, on my bed. I forbid them, even though I know they badly want to jump on it, but they know better. I have a shoe-free home, I don't want outdoor germs and dirt inside. I don't leave dirty dishes in the sink in the evening and wash or load them into the dishwasher the next morning. I wouldn't be

---

[71]. O'Sullivan, Megan. "The Psychology Of What's Inside Your Home." *Lonny.com*, Livingly Media, 19 Jan. 2019, lonny.com/See+It+Now/articles/7oMPDSAqAKc/Psychology+Inside+Home

able to sleep thinking about them sitting in the sink with scraps of food. How gross! I don't let my kids play indoors with modeling compound, paint, or anything else messy. I often hear them say "you're not fun." I don't care. I don't need to be fun. I need to be clean. I make sure every single toy is put away before going to bed each night. I want the house in order just in case I don't feel well and must be hospitalized (yes, I'm catastrophizing the future) at least everything will be where it needs to be. I know, I know, there are no words.

I grew up this way. As a child, I had a super clean home (even though my mother worked full-time as a seamstress for a wedding dress designer). It was filled with memorable things that were always in their correct place. Every time my mother went to Italy she would return with some piece of décor, including sketch prints of her hometown, a pink Murano lamp, a set of three striped, area rugs, and wool blankets. She taught me to do more than just eat and sleep at home, but to care about the small things and pay attention to details. I'm like my mother. I have in some ways unknowingly become her. I'm away from my home country working to build a familiar, safe place, a home, in what is a foreign land, just like she started doing when she arrived in America in 1969.

It took a while, but I do feel I have created a real home for my family in Germany. I know from the few visits I made to the apartments/homes of Italian wives that they didn't care much about building a home here. They brought little from their homes in Italy and got by thriftily with whatever they could find/buy second hand for their time in Germany. I couldn't live like that for four years but that's me. I couldn't put our home life on hold, especially because anything could happen. I wanted my things, my memories, with me. I needed to feel safe and happy in my home. I knew that I would have to take everything down when we moved. Pack it all up, and create another home, but I would worry about all that later.

There are other podcasts that I listen to in the health and wellness genre, but they offer more practical, hands-on advice on how to care for my physical body and feel less crappy. I am fixated on the food I eat and want advice on what's good and what's not so good. I have seen many different approaches to healthy eating. The Italians believe that carbs, in particular pasta, is the only real way to feed and heal your body. The Germans feel like they are eating a balanced meal because they put 15 peas on the same plate with a pork knuckle. The Americans are extremists, if they learn that something is "bad" they cut it out completely with no sugar, no carbs, no gluten, or no meat diets. I was helped to make more informed, better choices about my food thanks to the *Nutrition Diva* podcast. The show's host, nutritionist Monica Reinagel, separates fact from fiction using a simple scientific approach to explain topics like: Should we eat fewer eggs? What oils are best for high heat cooking? How dangerous is it really to eat red meat? In her weekly 10-minute episodes, she cuts through the conflicting nutrition news (and there is a lot of that out there) without using a lot of confusing jargon.

I also listen to Ella Mills' podcast called *Wellness with Ella*. The English wellness expert started with a blog in 2012 and now her portfolio includes books, food products, and a podcast. Mills is the daughter of British labour politician Shaun Woodward and Camilla Sainsbury, of the Sainsbury supermarket family. I love Sainsbury's supermarkets. I always stop at one when I'm in the UK, even if I don't really need anything in particular. I just like to look around. The chain reminds me of my favorite American big box store Target. In 2018, Mills started hosting the podcast with her husband Matthew. The weekly episodes are interview driven and include experts who provide their know-how on topics that include anything in the health and wellness space, such as living on a plant-based diet, sleep, calories, irregular menstrual cycles, and skincare. I have learned a lot from her guests about how to live a healthier life. She generously gives a lot of space to them, it's more about them than her, and it feels as if she is learning along with us listeners.

The episode "How to have a Healthy Gut"[72] was a 48-minute talk about bloating, gas, constipation, irritable bowel syndrome, and heartburn. I was completely into it because I want a healthy gut. I want my nine meter, or 30 foot, long digestive tract to function well.

---

72. Mills, Ella, host. "How to have a healthy gut." *Wellness with Ella*. Season 4, Episode 2, 24 Sept. 2019, deliciouslyella.com/podcast/how-to-have-a-healthy-gut/#play

Dr. Meghan Rossi, also known as The Gut Health Doctor, explained that 70 percent of our immune cells are in our digestive tract, which means that a healthy gut means a healthier life. The problem is that I don't always feel good when it comes to my gut. I complained to my general practitioner in GK about it on a few occasions but instead of reassuring me that everything was okay and not to worry (which was what I wanted him to do) he suggested I get a colonoscopy. The word colonoscopy made me nauseous. I asked, like a child, "Do I have to?" I suggested a stool exam: Wouldn't that be good enough? But he said no.

This is a country where the colon, the gut, was given spotlight attention, thanks to Giulia Enders, whose 2012 presentation *Darme mit Charme* (Charming Bowels) won her first prize at the Science Slam in Berlin and went viral on YouTube. She then went on to turn it into an international bestseller which came out in English as *Gut: The Inside Story of Our Body's Most Underrated Organ.* My GP was the thorough kind, he was never "let's wait and see" but instead "let's get this test." I was only in my very early 40s. I had never heard of 41-year-olds getting colonoscopies unless there was something suspect and wrong. I self-diagnosed. I was mortified. I read about all the things they could find during this endoscopic exam of my colon. I went for a pre-visit and scheduled the exam for Thursday, 28 November, 8:45 a.m. I knew it was the fourth Thursday of the month, which for me was a holiday, it was Thanksgiving. I couldn't explain this to the secretary (language issues) and she wouldn't care about my favorite American holiday. I didn't have many options. I didn't want to have the exam during the upcoming Christmas holidays, I didn't want to wait until the new year and so I agreed.

The thing is that I've always celebrated Thanksgiving, no matter where I was, it was important to reflect upon the year, be thankful, and yeah, eat turkey! In Italy, I always found a way to celebrate even though it was hard to find a whole bird. I asked my local butcher for a *tacchino intero* and she said they could order me a free range one. The turkey they could get me, though, would be about 18 kilos. I did the conversion and that was about 40 pounds — it was huge! I wouldn't be able to wash it in my kitchen sink and it definitely wouldn't fit in my small oven. I had to eat out, which was by American standards considered horrific on this holiday, but that seemed to be my only choice. I searched online and found a few places that catered to American expats on Thanksgiving, one in particular caught my attention, a small restaurant on the outskirts of Rome owned by an Italian-American woman. I booked in advance (you had to) and off I went with Marco, my then boyfriend. The turkey was juicy, the sweet potatoes were tender and moist, the herby stuffing was savory, and the ambiance was small and homey. I was satisfied, even happy, and it became my yearly Thanksgiving tradition in Italy. I can't say it was like Thanksgiving in New York, but it was nice.

In GK, there are many American service families and a Thanksgiving meal was held on the base. The American contingent organized a potluck celebration with all the traditional trimmings and so much more. It was nice even though most of the participants were strangers to me. But when I found ten-pound frozen Butterball turkeys from America for sale at the GK base supermarket, I decided to start my own tradition at home. I made my first traditional Thanksgiving dinner in Germany and invited two of my husband's Italian colleagues and their families to celebrate with us. There was no performance pressure for me because Italians know nothing about Thanksgiving, except what they have seen on television, and I was in my warm, comfortable turkey-smelling home. The celebration was a big success, at least I thought so when my husband's colleagues took selfies with the bird.

But in the year of my colonoscopy, I was agitated and sad. I wouldn't be celebrating Thanksgiving. I couldn't cook a turkey and host a dinner after the procedure. I didn't think I would feel up to going to the GK base celebration, and moreover I thought I might die on Thanksgiving of all days. I thought I might not see my kids again. I kissed them and hugged them so tightly the morning of my exam. I got to the doctor's office, and they took me into the exam room right away and then I was out of the exam room in what also seemed like an instant. I don't remember much in between but I do remember feeling the sensation of being tugged and pulled. I was told after the exam that everything was good, but that I had a "very twisty" gut. I wouldn't need another colonoscopy for at least 15 years. I was relieved and knew what I was thankful for that year. I bought Dr.

Rossi's book *Eat Yourself Healthy* and have tried to implement some of her suggestions into my daily life. So that's me: The girl with the twisty gut.

Another thing that helps me feel good is to make sleep a priority. The *Wellness with Ella* podcast episode about why we sleep[73] reaffirmed my commitment. Matthew Walker, a neuroscientist and sleep researcher, described sleep as a "life support system," and added that no matter what ailment we have "sleep can help." I believe that. I mentioned already that I need my shuteye. I go to sleep early to get my seven, eight hours each night. I have always put sleep first. I remember spending my summers in my parents' small seaside town and in the evenings the locals would retreat to the *piazza* and have a *gelato* or *granita*, and so did we. I tried to stay awake and have fun in the loud, brightly lit town square that had a carousel and other rides, but my need for sleep was stronger. I would bury my face in my arms on the café table where my parents were seated and talking to family and friends. I was happy when my father picked me up, placed my head on his shoulder, and carried me back to my grandparents' home.

I continued to put sleep first even as an adult. I'm really not nerdy. I've never pulled an all-nighter in college to study or write a paper. I preferred not to go to the movies late at night because I tended to fall asleep after about 15 minutes — it's dark and conducive to sleeping! I've missed the endings of a lot of movies. I even slept through the Broadway musical *Cats*. I used to sleep a lot on planes, but that was before I had kids. I loved falling asleep on transatlantic flights before takeoff. I would fall asleep while queuing on the tarmac and would wake up in Europe. I can't do that anymore, which stinks. In addition, I'm not nice at night. I get upset pretty easily, and that's why it's important for me to stick to my sleep schedule.

The only time I forcibly strayed from my sleep schedule was when my children were newborns. I suffered terribly during the night feedings, it was (curse word) horrible! I was a walking mess. I was

---

73. Mills, Ella, host. "Why we sleep with Matthew Walker." *Wellness with Ella*. Season 3, Episode 7, 18 June 2018, deliciouslyella.com/podcast/why-we-sleep-with-matthew-walker/

mentally and physically exhausted. I wanted to bond and cuddle with my babies, but during the day, not at night. I would feed them during the wee hours and focus on the image of the Virgin and Child above my bed and beg her to help them to fall back asleep as quickly as possible. Please Mary. And while I do prioritize sleep there are many times when I struggle.

In the *Wellness with Ella* episode Walker talked about the main reasons for insomnia, including technology and diet. He pointed to a study that said the use of screens decreases the hormone melatonin, which regulates our sleep-wake cycle. I'm raising my hand. I'm guilty. I use my phone at night. I use my phone in bed, but not to engage with social media. I mostly listen to podcasts. I don't want to give that up even though it's considered too stimulating. I don't consume alcohol regularly, which I learned fragments your sleep, but I do ingest a good amount of caffeine, mostly coffee, throughout the day. To get a good night's sleep, Walker suggested cutting off caffeine 12 to 14 hours before you expect to go to bed. If I want to be in bed at 9:30-10:00 p.m. I would have to stop drinking coffee at 10:00 a.m. I can't do that, or I will feel weak and begin feeling tired for the rest of the day. The thing is I don't want to feel crappy. I want to feel good about myself and good physically. I'm comforted by these podcasts because it's like I'm getting feedback from a friend with a little more experience, an older, wiser person. But they're not didactic, they don't tell me what to do. I love that. They educate my perspective and feelings by sharing first-hand knowledge and reminding me of the bigger picture.

List, listen, cross through. Archive.

I'm a list person. I'm list dependent. I write all different kinds of handwritten lists to help organize my life and yes, even some of my podcast listening is also organized into lists. I have a lot of shows I can't wait to get to. I write down the longform, storytelling podcasts I want to listen to and in what order. A bit extreme, I know, but that's me. I think my need for list writing, along with my love of good, moving stories, are why I enjoy limited series storytelling podcasts so much.

So what are limited series storytelling podcasts? These are not the quick daily news podcasts that give me an update of what's going on in the world and continue day-after-day like *NPR's Up First*, *BBC's Global News Podcast*, and *The New York Times' The Daily* (they don't need to be on my lists because they are always there) what I'm talking about here are storytelling podcasts that have a beginning, middle, and end. They run for a fixed period of time, or a certain number of episodes, and then they're over. They're done. The hosts and producers of these podcasts tell one story in however many episodes they need and then they are finished. They are not reaching or searching for another story that's just as good, or possibly better, for another episode or even another season. They draw it to a close and hopefully, if I like their work, they move on and put together another podcast about another great story with of course a different name. If there is a follow up, which is rare, it's only if something important, or big, has happened to advance the original story. I especially like the finished, all done, part. I'm happy that these podcasts, which require a significant commitment of time on my part, end and that I can cross them off one of my lists. I categorize them in a way.

The idea of a storytelling podcast that goes on week after week like a TV or radio show agitates me. I think, "when will it be over, when will it come to a close." I remember my work as a young journalist in New York and later in Rome. I liked the talking to people part. I had fun digging and doing research. I was happy to write the story and put it all together. I liked taking pictures and shooting video, if needed. I appreciated the editing. But then I wanted it to end. I wanted to be done, I wanted to file the story away and start something new. I needed closure, the all-done aspect.

I actually think it's quite courageous when podcasters say "yes, we're done," especially when they have the attention of their listeners. "Quit while you're ahead," is good advice in my view. Look at the wildly popular podcast *Serial* that I mentioned earlier. The first season, which made its debut in 2014, is considered the most successful US podcast of all time in terms of audience numbers, and a great example of the media's potential and reach. The podcast reinvestigated the case of Adnan Syed, who was convicted of first-degree murder for the 1999 killing of Hae Min Lee, a high school senior and Syed's classmate. He served more than 20 years in prison before prosecutors decided to drop all charges against him after advanced DNA testing ruled out Syed.

Hosted and executive produced by Sarah Koenig, *Serial* was filled with drama and intrigue and kept its audience glued to their podcast feed waiting for each of the 12 episodes to drop. *Serial* was the first podcast to hit five million downloads on Apple's iTunes,[74] and according to Serial Productions, the show has been downloaded 175 million times.[75] That's huge. I've listened to *Serial* several times, first for my own entertainment. I love stories, and a good one is always a good one, no matter what the media form. I learned all about this murder during my commute from Latina to Rome. I often listened standing with my headphones, but on those days my legs weren't so

---

74. Dredge, Stuart. "Serial podcast breaks iTunes records as it passes 5m downloads and streams." *The Guardian*, 18 Nov. 2014, theguardian.com/technology/2014/nov/18/serial-podcast-itunes-apple-downloads-streams

75. Spangler, Todd. "The 'Serial' Team's New Podcast, 'S-Town,' Tops 10 Million Downloads in Four Days." *Variety*, 31 March 2017, variety.com/2017/digital/news/s-town-podcast-10-million-downloads-serial-productions-1202020302/

achy, and the delays didn't seem that bad. I continued to listen as I slowly walked to my car, buckled up, and drove the less than two kilometers home. I forgot that I had been out of the house for 12 hours and if needed I sat in my car for 10 or so minutes to finish an episode. I couldn't wait until the next morning. I was later able to reexamine some episodes of *Serial* because I used it as a case study for my students in Rome. We studied it looking at the style and the content, and like me, most of them were really into it and had their own theories/ideas about what happened on that day in 1999. They liked the approach to storytelling and found it was a powerful way to tell a story in audio form.

But what about Season 2 and later Season 3? This is where the decline began. Hold on, I'm not saying that Season 2 and Season 3 were poorly made, they're not, but they didn't have the edginess and tension that made Season 1 what it was. In 2015, *Serial* Season 2, told the story of Sergeant Bowe Bergdahl who walked off his base in Afghanistan and was taken prisoner by the Taliban for five years. Bergdahl was released only after the U.S. government agreed to release five Taliban leaders from Guantánamo Bay in exchange for his freedom. I now eat up stories about military operations. I give credit to my husband for this somewhat newfound interest that developed in my 30s. I've watched every possible television series and film about them. I even listened to a few episodes of *Covert,* a podcast about international espionage and top-secret military operations hosted by Jamie Renell. I had already heard of the Bergdahl story since it was covered exhaustively by the mainstream media. The podcast's 11 episodes added more to the story and even asked a central question: Did anyone die in the search for Bergdahl? The answer, according to the podcast, was no. And while Season 2 won a Radio Television Digital News Association award for a news series, there were, however, no cliffhangers that kept me guessing, no edge of my seat anticipation, and no real drama to keep my attention strong throughout. I found my commute to be exhausting. I hated standing. I didn't sit in my car listening anymore. I would finish the episode later.

Then in 2018, *Serial* Season 3 changed its format. Instead of "one story, told week by week," which was its tagline, the podcast explored a series of singular criminal justice stories from inside the Cuyahoga County Justice Center in Cleveland, Ohio. The central theme was not a single story but instead the location. The Season 3 trailer still teased the story of Adnan Syed — they knew how fantastic it was — but Koenig explained that it was not a typical case and it didn't show how the criminal justice system worked. To do that she said *Serial* needed to look at "ordinary cases," and therefore they decided to look at the "entire criminal justice system." Is that even possible? Is one year inside the criminal courts in Cleveland the entire criminal justice system? I don't think so, I found the line quite grandiose. I also didn't listen right away. I put it on my list of podcasts to listen to, but it didn't push any of my other storytelling podcasts down.

Season 3 episodes told the stories of single cases, the ones filling up the dockets in judicial systems across America. The cases were interesting, but less dramatic. The pace was a lot faster as most things wrapped up in the about hour-long episodes. And while the consensus among podcast reviewers was that Season 3 was "an extraordinary accomplishment,"[76] and its "most ambitious"[77] season, especially because it continued to chase down complex stories, for me it was disappointing. Yes, it's innovative and avant-garde of *Serial* to use a different structure, but I expected a serialized narrative. I mean, it's called *Serial*, and the original idea was to tell a story in a serialized format. The fact that every episode of Season 1 and even some episodes of Season 2 were like a chapter of a story, one that I was excited to move through, is what made me stay from start to finish.

I found Season 3 to be choppy, fragmented, and even disconnected. I could pick and choose the episodes I wanted to listen to, and I wouldn't be lost if I skipped one or two. I didn't have to listen to all nine episodes. I did, but I took my time. I didn't listen on the day or even week the episodes dropped. And then I was like "Who's this?" when I heard a new British voice on the podcast, a

---

76. Loofbourow, Lili. "The Extraordinary Accomplishment of Serial Season 3." *Slate*, 18 Oct. 2018, slate.com/culture/2018/10/serial-season-3-cleveland-criminal-justice.html

77. Nicolaou, Elena. "Why Season 3 Of Serial Is The Most Ambitious One Yet." *Refinery29*, Vice Media Group, 20 Sept. 2018, refinery29.com/en-us/2018/09/210458/serial-season-3-about-cleveland-criminal-justice-system

reporter/producer named Emmanuel Dzotsi. I like British accents. I especially like my daughter's, which she interestingly uses on an as-needed basis, around her British teachers and friends. I was surprised because I expected Koenig. Plus, Dzotsi's presence wasn't consistent. His voice disappeared for an episode or two and then reappeared in bits and pieces. Sure, I do have some Type A personality characteristics. I am stressed, work obsessed, sometimes impatient, but I don't have permanently tight lips or a clenched jaw. I'm not an overly rigid person who hates to change and doesn't adjust well to it. I'm flexible. I just didn't get what I wanted or expected from *Serial*.

I am a big compare-and-contrast person. I have always been. As a teenager, I compared MTV's Season 1 of the reality show *The Real World* to Season 2 and Season 3 and then I stopped watching. And who didn't compare the films *The Karate Kid* or *Rocky* to their many sequels, most of which were one big disappointment after another. But it's not just me here. The science says we always remember the bad over the good. There are many studies that suggest we are more likely to remember more clearly and vividly negative experiences over positive ones. In an interview with *Time* magazine[78] Matt Wilson, a professor of neurobiology at MIT's Picower Institute for Learning and Memory, explained that we remember unpleasant events more because "the idea is not just to store information; it's to store relevant information. [The idea is] to use our experience to guide future behavior." So *Serial's* Season 2 and Season 3 have damaged my memory of Season 1. They are still on my podcast list, but will I revisit it? I doubt it.

Not all podcasts disappoint me in the second and third season. *The Dropout*, is a limited series storytelling podcast about Elizabeth Holmes and her biotech startup called Theranos. I listened to Episode 1 and 2 and thought, "I need to call my sister and tell her about this great story and podcast." I looked at the clock, but it was only 5:00 a.m. in New York — too early to call. I had to wait. I do that a lot

---

78. Blue, Laura. "Why Do We Remember Bad Things?" *Time,* 23 June 2008, content.time.com/time/health/article/0,8599,1817329,00.html

throughout my day. I look at my watch, my phone, or the microwave and take away six hours. I'm here but I also want to be there in Eastern Standard Time. I'm always a little happier when it's officially Springtime and the clocks are moved forward one hour in Europe, but New York is still in Wintertime for at least another week. That means there are only five hours between us and I can call everyone I need to earlier in my day. But talking to my sister about *The Dropout*, had to wait.

Hosted by Rebecca Jarvis and produced by ABC Radio and Nightline (part of Walt Disney Television) *The Dropout*, is a fascinating business story of mystery and intrigue. Holmes, once a Silicon Valley darling, was the youngest self-made female billionaire. After less than two years of college, she dropped out of Stanford University, hence the name of the podcast, to launch her company in 2003. Theranos, she claimed, could detect hundreds of diseases from a pinprick of blood. She was considered revolutionary in the healthcare technology field and was heralded as the next Steve Jobs. She even had his signature black turtleneck look. Holmes raised $1 billion in venture capital funding from high profile investors, including Rupert Murdoch and Betsy DeVos. But behind the scenes the company's technology didn't deliver. Her patented blood tests gave inaccurate results. Holmes was convicted of three counts of wire fraud and one count of conspiracy to commit wire fraud by lying to investors to raise money for her company. She was sentenced to an 11-year prison term.

The story, told in just six moving episodes, is a well reported account of how the rich and powerful were duped by Holmes. There is no editorializing from Jarvis; she sticks to traditional reporting, she asks direct questions, and provides listeners with facts and details. She lets her sources give their opinions; we don't hear hers. This approach is somewhat rare in news or storytelling podcasting, where many hosts take advantage of the freedom the media offers to insert and often share personal thoughts and ideas about what they are talking about or reporting on.

I was really into this podcast. I even did my own research after the episodes. I wanted to know more. I heard a lot about Holmes's signature look — thin figure and blond hair — and about how mesmerizing she was. I did, of course, want to see what she looked like. Was she really this vision? I wouldn't call her an Aphrodite but definitely pretty. I also thought how great it was that the podcast did more than recycle and repackage existing reporting in a new media form. Former *Wall Street Journal* reporter John Carreyrou broke the story in 2015[79] and put the first spotlight on the company and its claims. In 2018, Carreyrou released the book *Bad Blood. Secrets and Lies in a Silicon Valley Startup* that chronicled Theranos's rise and fall. Jarvis interviewed Carreyrou and used his knowledge of Holmes and Theranos to fill in the story. I requested Carreyrou's book from the local U.S. Army's Military Library, which all NATO members here have access to, and they got a copy for me. I'm always amazed by the U.S. military's logistics; they provide a lot for their service members and families abroad. There are exclusive interviews with former Theranos staff and family members but what makes the podcast noteworthy is its access to never-before-released deposition tapes. I was taken aback by the raw footage of Holmes being questioned about Theranos and her relationships. In an interview Jarvis said that her team started to understand that with the deposition tapes they had found something that was "truly unique" in the story.[80] The material from the tapes undercut interviews and public statements that Holmes and Theranos made and showed a whole different side. I heard Holmes' signature baritone voice and her quick answers — "I don't know," "no" and "not to my knowledge." I found the vague responses frustrating and was getting annoyed with her. I wished they would have pushed her a bit, even though I know that's not what happens during depositions. I still, though, wanted to listen and that's why *The Dropout* stayed on my listening list.

I also found the *BBC World Service* podcast *The Hurricane Tapes* to be a compelling limited series podcast. The 13-episode podcast

---

79. Carreyrou, John. "Hot Startup Theranos Has Struggled With Its Blood-Test Technology." *The Wall Street Journal,* 16 Oct. 2015, wsj.com/articles/theranos-has-struggled-with-blood-tests-1444881901

80. Liptak, Andrew. "ABC's podcast series The Dropout explores the downfall of Theranos and Elizabeth Holmes." *The Verge,* Vox Media, 10 Feb. 2019, theverge.com/2019/2/10/18216012/dropout-podcast-abc-series-theranos-elizabeth-holmes

reexamined from almost every point of view the case of Rubin "Hurricane" Carter, a world-famous middleweight boxer who was accused, alongside John Artis, of a triple homicide at the Lafayette Bar in Paterson, New Jersey, in June 1966. In the early morning hours two black men walked into the shoddy bar and in about 20 seconds shot four white people. Carter and Artis were arrested because they fitted an eyewitness description of the killers — two black men in a white car with New York state license plates. They were found guilty, but their convictions were overturned on two separate occasions. The American judicial system never ruled conclusively on who carried out the bar room murders. Their plight was documented in the protest song "Hurricane" by Bob Dylan released in 1976 and was also the subject of a 1999 Hollywood film starring Denzel Washington.

Hosted and produced by Steve Crossman and Joel Hammer, the podcast promised to tell the "full story" of what happened, while also trying to help solve the more than 50-year-old case. The story unfolded episode-by-episode in a compelling, but casual style. The language, British accents included, was hip and chatty, and often accompanied with excerpts from Dylan's "Hurricane" song. The amicable conversations that the hosts/producers had with their sources were included, along with quirky moments and the faux pas. Here too, though, it's the exclusive audio — 40 hours of never before heard recordings of Carter, who died in 2014 — that made the podcast powerful. The recordings were cassette tapes of Carter in conversation with Ken Klonsky, co-author of the book *Eye of the Hurricane: My Path from Darkness to Freedom*. The content from the tapes, the Carter soundbites, were an important part of the podcast. They were long and free of limits and time constraints. I heard Carter ramble. I heard him talk about his spirituality. I heard his desperation. I heard the rage and anger in his voice. I thought, "wow, this guy was intense."

From the start, Crossman told listeners that unlike other BBC World Service productions, "we are going to reach our own conclusions" and it was a type of warning to listeners that the podcast was going to be opinionated. He often used the words "we," "our," and "I" and their use tugged at the podcast's sense of impartiality. I was, though, surprisingly not scandalized by this. I usually would be,

I'm quite the disciplinarian when it comes to objectivity, at least when it's from something that wants to be called journalism. I'm old school that way. I teach that to my journalism students. Yet the reporting in this story — one whole year's worth — was a fair and honest account of what happened. I didn't mind the occasional editorializing as it still left room for my own ideas. I was hooked until the end but pleased when it was complete. That's how endings should be.

Another limited series podcast that made it on to my list was *Man in the Window*. Produced by the *Los Angeles Times* and *Wondery*, the podcast told the story of the "Golden State Killer" who raped and murdered his way through California in the 1970s and 1980s. He preyed on communities throughout the state, often stalking his victims through their bedroom windows. He first attacked women alone at home with their children, but later the list of victims expanded to couples in their homes. In April 2018, some 40 years after his first attack, police identified Joseph DeAngelo, a Vietnam veteran and former police officer, as the "Golden State Killer." Through genetic profiling using crime-scene DNA, DeAngelo's name emerged from what was a pool of possible suspects. They then matched a discarded DNA sample from his home and the connection was made.

I learned about *Man in the Window* from a daily email newsletter I subscribe to about podcasts. I'm usually in the know about big stories, but I must admit that before the podcast I had no idea about DeAngelo's horrific crimes. I was surprised, I couldn't believe I missed this story. Sure, I wasn't born when DeAngelo started his rape and killing spree, and when the story was unfolding in real time I was young and living on the opposite side of the United States. I do remember being little and overhearing my parents talk about the news, especially my Dad; he read a lot about everything. He taught himself how to read and write in English. He picked up a copy of *The New York Times* every Sunday. (Back then, it was beautifully thick and heavy, and as soon as I could handle a newspaper, he started to share the sections with me. I developed my love for journalism and stories thanks to him.)

But when it came to serial killers, I recall my parents talking about David Berkowitz, best known as the Son of Sam, who terrorized New

Yorkers in the late 1970s. I remember them saying that more and more people in Brooklyn were armed. This came vividly to light in one family incident. To give my mother a break after a long day, my father would drive my brothers around Bensonhurst, what was then a mostly Irish and Italian neighborhood. The boys were in the backseat with their printed pajamas on and usually after about 10-minutes they were fast asleep, which meant they could be carried straight into bed. But on one evening drive, a double-parked car on Bay 47, between 86th Street and Benson Avenue, was preventing my father's brown Buick Regal from passing through. He rolled down the window and asked the driver to move. My older brother, who was probably seven or eight years old at the time, jumped up from the back and beeped the horn. The driver got out of the car, went up to my father and pointed a gun at him. My father was shaken up, and said, "I have two kids in the back, just let me go." The man nodded and said, "get out of here." In Brooklyn, when guns are involved, small incidents can have tragic consequences.

But the DeAngelo story was new to me. Luckily, I caught up with the whole story thanks to the podcast. Hosted by *Los Angeles Times* reporter Paige St. John, the podcast fed my interest for real-life cases. It not only detailed the rapes and murders but also looked at how men and women treated sexual assault, how the survivors and perpetrators were viewed in the 1970s and 1980s, and how these types of cases were investigated.

St. John, a Pulitzer Prize winner, used her solid reporting and writing skills and landed exclusive interviews with detectives who worked the case back in the 1970s and with many of the surviving victims, including Bonnie Colwell. The podcast was Colwell's first interview with the media since she was identified as DeAngelo's former fiancée. This was the "Bonnie" that the "Golden State Killer" sobbed about after one attack in 1978. "I hate you, Bonnie," her rapist cried into the pillow in July 1978. The storytelling in the podcast was filled with testimony, vivid descriptions, and authentic soundscapes.

In the podcast, St. John talked about the "Golden State Killer's" first victim, Phyllis Zitka, who was 23 years old at the time. She provided a compelling explanation with even certain parts acted out. St. John said Zitka woke up to a "tap, tap, tap." She thought it was her father but instead it was the "Golden State Killer" who said to her that if she made one move or sound he would kill her. She then provided intimate details: "The man in Phyllis' bedroom moves fast, he collects things to tie her up — her small robe, a cloth belt, a bra, and the electric cord from her hair dryer. He gags her with her slip and binds her so tight the circulation is cut off. And he presses a knife to her temple." St. John explained that the "Golden State Killer" raped and sodomized Zitka. He didn't leave, though, she said. He ransacked her room. He whispered to himself, argued to himself. Zitka heard him hiss loudly, "I told you to shut up." This all acted out. And the podcast also used a recording of a phone call the "Golden State Killer" made to Zitka after the attack. There was heavy breathing and then the haunting words, "I am going kill you, I am going to kill you. Bitch, bitch, bitch, bitch. Fucking whore."

And while some of these details are chilling, I didn't find the podcast to be irresponsible or exploitative. I didn't feel like it was trying to scare or invoke fear in me, as horrible as it all was, it's a true crime podcast. *Man in the Window* puts the pieces of a real, complicated story together. I didn't want to stop listening. I wanted to keep going. I wouldn't call it an audio version of a television murder investigation, but the podcast used elements of drama in its narrative storytelling approach, in particular the scene setting and acting out of parts, the intense musical underscore, and the cliffhangers at the end of each episode.

These limited series storytelling podcasts, and there are so many more of them, give me my great story fix, keep me updated about big, important news stories so that when I get out of here, I don't act as if I have been in a coma for four years. They also appease my need for a sense of completion, an accomplishment, or you know, crossing out items on my lists. I can't explain how happy I feel when I draw a solid, thick line through podcast titles that I have listened to. I need order. I'm the person who if I complete something that's not on my list, I write it down and then immediately cross it through. I can't have an item completed without the satisfaction of the solid line. Plus, the lists are proof of what I have achieved on a certain day, week, or month. I have an office cabinet filled with small notebooks with completed lists inside. I guess I save them for my own personal amusement — look at all the things I have done, yeah! — but I do think that one day I might need to refer to them. It's my own personal handwritten archive.

There is, though, a ton of theory and evidence that shows that unfulfilled goals and tasks, like the podcasts in my app and the ones on my lists, persist and occupy the human mind. This is the Zeigarnik effect.[81] Russian psychologist Bluma Zeigarnik first stumbled upon the psychological phenomenon while sitting in a restaurant in Vienna. She noticed that the busy and frantic waiters seemed to only remember orders in the process of being served, but once they were completed, the order seemed to disappear from their memories. To study this, Zeigarnik asked a number of people in a lab to do a series of simple tasks, such as solve a puzzle or string beads. A few of the participants were interrupted half-way through the tasks and afterwards Zeigarnik asked them which activities they remembered doing. She found that people were twice as likely to remember the tasks during which they had been interrupted than those completed.

Meanwhile, a more recent study from Wake Forest University[82] showed that even though the tasks we haven't done distract us, just planning to get them done can free us from all the anxiety. Professors E. J. Masicampo and Roy F. Baumeister found that people underperformed on a task when they are unable to finish a warm-up activity that would usually precede it. However, when they were allowed to make specific plans for their warm-up activity performance their next task improved substantially. The point: plan making, like list writing, helps to see a goal through to completion. For me, that means a great number of podcasts follow the pattern of list, listen, cross through, and archive.

---

81. Vinney, Cynthia. "What Is the Zeigarnik Effect? Definition and Examples." *ThoughtCo*, DotdashMeredith, 30 Sept. 2019,.thoughtco.com/zeigarnik-effect-4771725

82. Masicampo, E.J. and Roy F. Baumeister. "Consider It Done! Plan Making Can Eliminate the Cognitive Effects of Unfulfilled Goals." *Journal of Personality and Social Psychology*, 20 June 2011, doi: 10.1037/a0024192

Eating in

When my general practitioner asked me where I went out to eat good Italian food, I thought about it for a few seconds and then shrugging I said, "I don't know. I don't really go out to eat much anymore." I'm not happy about this but that's just the way it is for me here because this is certainly not a country of gastronomy. I figured I'd start eating out again when I moved out of here, which was only a matter of time.

In Italy, I went out often and there were a lot of delicious choices. I ate exceptionally well at restaurants, trattorias, and pizzerias, as well as snack bars and food trucks. Even the service station restaurants and cafés dotted along Italian highways and in airport terminals had lots of tempting snacks and sandwiches. I especially enjoyed peering through the glass of the display case and looking at what was on offer that day. I usually went with what was called a *rustichella*, a flatbread sandwich with smoked bacon, sharp provolone, and oregano, and nodded fervently when I was asked if I wanted it heated up a bit — of course, I did.

In Rome, I had a few favorite places, places where I was regular, where they knew me, where they called me by name or simply *bella* when I walked in. I often ate at a small trattoria in the artsy Garbatella neighborhood, where I first lived when I moved to Italy. The trattoria was homey and laid back with an odd equestrian-themed decor — imagine horses in photographs, paintings, and statues everywhere — but that didn't matter much. This was the type of place where the menu was unnecessary; they did have a few but they were for tourists who didn't understand the trattoria concept. That wasn't me anymore. The waiter, who was the owner, would look down at his scrappy, stapled together notepad and read off the day's specials, and I would just choose one of those sure-to-be delicious options. I always found the dishes, such as the *pasta e fagioli* (pasta and beans), homemade *gnocchi al ragu* (gnocchi with meat sauce), as well as the *involtini alla romana* (rolled stuffed veal) and the *polpette con sugo* (meatballs with sauce) to be good, genuine, just like home cooking, but better because there was no work involved on my part. And while the trattoria was casual, I couldn't just decide on a whim to eat there, the place was always packed and that meant reservations were needed.

For me as for many people, pizza Friday was a well-loved tradition. We either went out to one of our usual places or if we were too tired or the weather wasn't great we ordered in. I never, ever, made pizza at home; there was no need for it. There was of course Roman pizza and if we wanted Neapolitan pizza that was easily available too. We often went to a pizzeria run by genuine Neapolitans near Piazza del Popolo in the historic center. They made sure the dough was leavened for at least 24 hours and that all the necessary ingredients — tomatoes, cheese, meats — were sourced from their original Italian locations. The result: crispy pizza with a thick and airy crust that even my very picky Neapolitan husband enjoyed.

When it was time for *gelato*, I often went out of my way to an artisanal ice cream shop at Piazza Re de Roma in the San Giovanni neighborhood. The shop, which always had a line snaking out the door onto the sidewalk, only offered a half dozen flavors each day. There weren't multiple ice cream display cases filled with 150 flavors to choose from like Rome's famous Gelateria Della Palma.[83] Nice, but somewhat overwhelming. The *gelato* was made fresh each day with genuine ingredients. The pistachio, my favorite, was made with real pistachio nuts, along with local milk and cream, and sugar. The ingredients were written right there; talk about transparency.

I admit it, I was a food snob in Italy. The thing is I wasn't the only one acting somewhat pretentious; it was allowed, it was the norm. I felt like everyone was into food and could talk about it in a sophisticated kind-of-way. I even name-dropped chefs in casual conversations. I often mentioned that in my work as a journalist I had interviewed and tasted dishes from Michelin-rated chefs like Antonino Cannavacciuolo, who stars in the Italian version of

---

83. "Our 150 Flavors." *Gelateria della Palma*. dellapalma.it/the-150-tastes/?lang=en

MasterChef; Antonello Colonna, known for making Italian regional cooking a bit gourmet; and even internationally known pizza makers like Gino Sorbillo. I often got the "here we go again" look from my husband, but I liked telling these stories they were like a badge of honor. But all this didn't mean that I frowned at a juicy bacon cheeseburger with fries or a chocolate milkshake — I enjoyed them too, I was still American — but, as I said earlier, my palette had evolved in Italy.

I have always been, though, a measured realist. I understood that in Germany the food would be different. But I still thought Friday night pizza was possible because there were plenty of what I thought (and what were marketed) as Italian pizzerias and restaurants. They all went heavy with the red, white, and green decor (I soon learned, a bad sign) and had names like "Da Marco," "Da Nino," and "Da Pepe," but unfortunately there was very little Italian about them. The menus often had spelling mistakes, no *margherita* is not spelled like margarita the cocktail, and in some cases the pizza makers were trying to pass off as Italians. I walked into one local pizzeria and saw a picture of *"Michele, the pizzaiuolo,"* the pizza maker, hanging on the wall in an ornate, gold frame above the table where we were seated. I had never seen pizzamakers idolized like saints; this was weird. Later in the evening, Michele, the man from the picture, walked out of the kitchen and greeted the pizzeria's patrons — that's nice, I thought — but when Marco asked him in Italian where he was from, he couldn't answer. He later explained in English that his nickname was Michele. His real name was Mustafa and he was from Konya in Turkey.

I didn't order anything fancy or complicated at these pizzerias. I always went with a simple *pizza margherita*, you know with tomato and mozzarella. But after every pizza out I was either up at night drinking water because of all the salt or I needed ginger ale or something like an effervescent digestive aid. So, I was happily optimistic the night we went to a so-called Neapolitan pizzeria recommended by Mario, one of my husband's colleagues, who now lived permanently in GK. I thought, maybe this is it, maybe this is our Friday night place, maybe we could become regulars. I missed being a regular somewhere. I like routine.

I ordered my usual pizza but when it was placed in front of me, I thought the color of mozzarella looked a bit yellow, but I dismissed the thought and figured it was the fluorescent lighting. I cut my pizza into slices but when I tasted it, the mozzarella was off, it was strange. I asked the waiter about it. I had to, you understand, right? He told me that they used Gouda on their *pizza margherita* and that if I wanted mozzarella I needed to ask for it. What? I needed to request mozzarella on a *pizza margherita*? Gouda. Gouda! That's a mild, cow's milk cheese from the Netherlands. It's good, but on pizza, it's a no-no, it's sinful, just like pineapple on pizza. It's a food crime. If the Associazione Verace Pizza Napoletana,[84] a non-profit organization that works to promote and protect genuine pizza making in Italy and throughout the world, had heard about or seen this they would be fired up. I know that I was. The only ingredients for a *pizza margherita* are tomatoes, olive oil, mozzarella, a few basil leaves, and grated hard cheese. If they wanted to put Gouda on it then they needed to call it something else. I had overlooked the fact that Mario had been an expat for more than 10 years and tastes change.

    I didn't just try Italian pizzerias. I was even willing to turn Friday pizza into something else so long as we could eat out somewhere. I went to a few so-called Greek places (all named after cities or islands — Athens, Mykonos, Crete), Spanish places, Japanese places, and even a few local German restaurants, and was equally disappointed. I tried a burger and fries joint, and while the food was good, the black cat walking around while we were eating unsettled me. Then hours later at home Marco was wheezing and needed to use an emergency inhaler because being in the restaurant for an hour with a cat had triggered an asthmatic episode. I couldn't go back there again.

    And don't get me started on the damn bees. On the few days when it's warm and sunny, when it's perfect to sit outdoors and enjoy a meal or even a not so yummy ice cream, there are wild bees everywhere. The Germans oddly aren't bothered by them. They ignore them when they are flying close by or resting on their drinks or food; they don't even shoo them away. What? But we're different,

---

84. "International Regulation." *Associazione Verace Pizza Napoletana*, pizzanapoletana.org/en/ricetta_pizza_napoletana

we're afraid.

One time I brought the kids out for a sweet treat at a local café during the summer and the bees were all over, harassing us. My son was crying in my arms. My daughter was pushing them away with a paper napkin begging me to have the waitress move us to a table indoors. I didn't know what to do. I never had this problem in Italy or in America. I killed three of them. I had no other choice. I know bees are important. I know they pollinate a third of the world's food. I know it's not permissible to kill bees, hornets, or wasps without good reason, but our lives were a good enough reason for me. I saw the disapproving looks, the angry frowns, from the locals sitting nearby. I thought they would call the environmental *Polizei* on me. I had the kids finish up quickly and we ran out of there.

There came a time in GK after probably almost three years when I was done trying to find a good (and safe) place to eat. I had enough of eating out and being let down all the time, and feeling sick. I once got food poisoning at a local Portuguese restaurant. I resigned myself to my fate, to my family's fate. I gave up. I started to get some real use of my newly purchased standup kitchen mixer (with a C dough hook accessory). I started making pizza at home with Marco. I can't say our first pizzas were fantastic; some didn't grow enough; some had too much or too little salt. But they didn't make me feel sick after eating them. I learned that the craft of pizza making takes time because there's a lot of chemistry going on when it comes to the levitation of the dough. I supplemented my basic skills with information and tips from podcasts, which, as always in my life here in Germany, are there to help and assist me, and also keep me sane until it's time to leave.

I listened to the Italian language pizza podcast called *Lo Scassapizza*. The show, hosted by Antonio Fucito, is all about pizza. I scrolled through my feed to find episodes that could help me, such as the one specifically about making pizza at home.[85] Fucito talked about

---

85. Fucito, Antonio, host. "Pizza fatta in casa:qualche consiglio per la napoletana e in teglia." *Lo Scassapizza (Tanzen vs Pizza),* March 2020, open.spotify.com/episode/4ThaIp35za82aNfxGodOR0

understanding your oven — I definitely didn't understand my oven...I thought it was just bake or broil — because that will determine the kind of pizza you will make. For example, if you want a pizza that's crunchy and crispy then it's best to use the ventilated or fan function, but if you want a pizza cooked in a more uniform way, then go with the static oven function. He also focused on primary ingredients, especially the flour and yeast, noting that they make a difference, and each kind/amount will produce different results. After a lot, I mean a lot, of trial and error, Marco and I finally found that a mix of Italian OO flour, 70 percent, and whole wheat flour, 30 percent, with 70 percent hydration, the amount of water in relation to the amount of flour, produced the kind of pizza that we enjoyed.

I also listened to episodes of *Pizza Nerds*, a podcast exclusively about making pizza at home. The show, which has since stopped airing new episodes, was hosted by friends, Kendra Adachi and Michael Van Patter. That's one of the best things about podcasts, even if the show ends, you can always still access the episodes. I listened to the New York series, and I was able to mix my pizza style every once in a while with their recommended recipe that called for basic bread flour, water, salt, and olive oil. I did my best to stick to the process, kneading it for three minutes, before dividing it into balls, and then letting it rise for 24 hours. I also liked them because they gave me a lot of encouragement, as if they were providing a sort of support group for people trying to make pizza at home. Yes, it's hard, it really is! They even pointed out that "...there is no perfect pizza. The goal is to have fun and learn." I love them, I told you they were great. I did try to go the fancier route and turn our barbecue into a pizza oven with a metal box that sat on the top of the grill. The contraption was easy to use, but despite cleaning the grill and preheating it for longer than usual, the pizza smelled and tasted of what we had grilled the night before — sausages and steaks. What was I thinking? The following Friday, I went back to using the oven, which I now understood a little better.

The pizza making was in addition to everything else I was cooking most days of the week unless Marco was inspired to cook. I needed and wanted new ideas and guidance, especially because I had never been passionate about cooking. I like to eat more than I like to cook, but in GK I had to do more of it, a lot more. I shopped locally and found lots of cruciferous vegetables, like cabbage and Brussel sprouts, and root vegetables like turnips, beets, and kohlrabi (never heard or seen kohlrabi before moving to Germany). There were also tons and tons of potatoes. They sell three, five, or 10 kilo sacks from 24-hour vending machines here; just in case you need them after hours. Weird. I understood, the lack of sun and the cold meant they relied a lot on vegetables that grow underground but I still missed the variety I had in Rome and New York.

That's why I needed help from people who took food seriously, who understood it, and who knew how to best exploit ingredients — Italians. I searched for Italian food podcasts. I got an audio crash course about vegetables from the podcast *Mangia come parli*. The weekly show from Radio 24, an all-news radio station that produces and also repackages its broadcasts as podcasts, is part cooking tutorial, part gastronomic culture. I listened to a few episodes of the show that was hosted by chef Davide Oldani and journalist Pierluigi Pardo, and thought that these guys were doing this weekly show just for me — they must know that I'm here with these vegetables and that I don't know what the hell to do with them.

In an episode about cruciferous vegetables,[86] the hosts narrowed in on white cauliflower. In Italy, I avoided cooking white cauliflower because of its stinky smell, and often chose the purple one, but that wasn't available in GK. The hosts talked about its benefits and costs, and gave three recipes, including one for roasted white cauliflower. In a simple, straightforward way Oldani, a Michelin starred chef, suggested slicing the cauliflower and then cooking it slowly in butter until it was golden brown. He also said to take the leftover cauliflower parts and make a sauce by cooking them in a vegetable-based broth. He then said to puree them, add some olive oil, and grate the skin of an orange. He didn't provide precise measurements or amounts, but his explanations were thorough enough that I felt comfortable giving

---

86. Oldani, Davide and Pierluigi Pardo, hosts. "Il Cavolfiore." *Mangia come parli*, Radio24, 21 Nov. 2020, radio24.ilsole24ore.com/programmi/mangia-parli/puntata/il-cavolfiore-110516-ADUcQ92?refresh_ce=1

it a try without further instructions.

There was even an episode about celeriac.[87] I often see mountains of the big, ugly looking ball shaped vegetables waiting to be picked up in the farmland that surrounds our village. I always ignored it at the supermarket, but after Oldani and Pardo talked about its qualities and how it was making its way onto more and more tables in Italy, I decided to buy one. I made it the way Oldani suggested. I cleaned its whiskered patched, rough skin, drizzled it with olive oil and thyme, wrapped it in foil, and baked it in the oven. I was surprised that it tasted good. I actually liked its sweet, nutty flavor. I know, I'm weak, but I needed the Italians to tell and show me that it was edible. I needed an okay from people who know food. I later searched for other ways to cook celeriac and found that I could even make it with a long pasta, like spaghetti or linguine. I diced it into cubes and cooked it in a vegetable-based broth with minced carrots, celery, onions, and olives then tossed the cooked pasta in. I no longer look at root vegetables and tubers with disdain anymore.

The centerpiece and highlight of German cuisine is meat. The average annual consumption of meat in Germany is about 77 kg per person each year while Italy is at about 74 kg per person.[88] And there is a lot of it here. I've never had a problem finding a specific cut for say a beef soup, *Suppenfleisch,* or meat-based red sauce, *Hochrippe,* it's all quite plentiful and tastes good, really good. The bratwurst, or sausage, is so popular that there are German proverbs about it like "*Alles hat ein Ende, nur die Wurst hat zwei,*" which means "Everything has an ending but the sausage has two." The links of different sizes are displayed in a visually striking way sort of like candy in a sweet shop. They are strung from the ceiling on a rope, hung off big hooks, and even twirled in a giant glass jar. I especially liked the ones with *Käse*, cheese, in them. I feel like we've had our best barbecues here, at least from a meat perspective. I even added ćevapi to our menu. The

---

87. Oldani, Davide and Pierluigi Pardo, hosts. "Il Sedano Rapa." *Mangia Come Parli,* Radio24, 7 Nov. 2020, radio24.ilsole24ore.com/programmi/mangia-parli/puntata/il-sedano-rapa-110515-ADGl9G0

88. Hannah Ritchie, Pablo Rosado and Max Roser. "Meat consumption tends to rise as we get richer." *Our World in Data,* 2023, ourworldindata.org/meat-production

rolled minced meat is of Bosnian origin but I think the Germans have adopted it as it is sold in almost every meat market.

I wouldn't want to feed my family more than three servings of meat per week, but there isn't much of an alternative, at least not fish wise. The weekly, outdoor fish market is 25 km away in the Netherlands and it isn't always possible to be there first thing on a Thursday morning. The supermarkets, even the big superstores, only have one, small glass refrigerated case dedicated to seafood, usually with unappetizing cod and salmon. I had never really eaten much fresh salmon before coming to Germany. I mostly ate smoked salmon and in New York that meant on a bagel with cream cheese — delicious.

I grew up eating other kinds of seafood because my parents, who were born and raised in a fishing town, included it in my diet. In New York, part of my childhood was on Long Island. There, fish was everywhere with shops filled with local catch. They always had monkfish and whiting, which my mother used to make soup. There were mussels, but also all different size clams, which we often ate baked, steamed, or with pasta. I also liked crabs cooked in sauce. I enjoyed the porgies and striped bass, which we often grilled on the barbeque, and even baked, or fried fluke. I found more of the same in Italy. The species and sizes of the fish were a bit different, but the abundance of choice was the same.

I didn't have this in GK and needed more meatless ideas and turned to Giallo Zafferano, Italy's leading online cooking portal. They started a simple podcast in early 2020, right around the height of the first wave of the Covid-19 pandemic when more people were home cooking, in which they provided audio recipes. There is little to no chatter in the short three to four minutes episodes because they just get straight to the details, which I liked. I found their recipes easy to follow and their zucchini pie[89] (minus the bacon), rice salad,[90]

---

89. "Torta salata di Zucchine." *GialloZafferano: le Ricette,* Mondadori Media, June 2020, open.spotify.com/episode/777fdLBKdw3Tuta5WJR5Jt

90. "Insalata di Riso." *GialloZafferano: le Ricette,* Mondadori Media, April 2020, open.spotify.com/episode/7FwVnDWloZAotphrdAv5cL

mushroom risotto,[91] and chickpea pancake[92] are among the meatless dishes I now make for my family.

I didn't laugh when my husband joked that I was the village's winner for most trash produced — not funny — but it was clear why we produced so much garbage, especially the wet waste, the one that went in the brown bin and we paid for by kilo. It was because I cooked and my German neighbors didn't, or at least not as much as me. How did I know? From their garbage. Yes, I casually snooped around their curbside trash during my late afternoon neighborhood walks and got an idea about what they were eating. I had to, I was curious, you understand?

I found that most families in the village didn't put out their brown bin, and if they did, there was barely anything in it. I always had a full brown bin: food scraps, fruit and vegetable skins, eggshells, meat and some fish waste, coffee grinds, and my daily tea bags. But when it came to plastic and metal waste, I noticed they had a lot more. I saw through the yellow transparent bags and made out canned soup and vegetables and plastic packaging for all sorts of foods, especially for pre-sliced deli meats and cheeses. And their paper bins were filled with cardboard and cellulose take-away boxes, some bought from the store and some from local non-Italian pizzerias.

In my search for Italian food podcasts, I also came across something different, a six-episode podcast called *Lingua* by food blogger Mariachiara Montera. The podcast told stories about how people meet, how they leave each other, how they love each other, and how they care for each other thanks to food. I was hooked right from the introduction when Montera in an intense, yet inviting voice, explained that cooking and eating is the most frequent thing we do day in and day out, and even if we're not interested in it there is always a taste, a smell, an ingredient that brings back some memory.

Besides the great storytelling, I found that the series helped me to

---

91. "Risotto ai Funghi." *GialloZafferano: le Ricette,* Mondadori Media, March 2020, open.spotify.com/episode/7iOyS7fsZPDqZNb5pcWSgu

92. Farinata di Ceci." *GialloZafferano: le Ricette*, Mondadori Media, May 2020, open.spotify.com/episode/6lZ4sy9k7qsl5oxHecjzBf

remember a lot of my memories tied to food, in particular those about eating out. I remember day trips with my parents to Montauk Point, the easternmost part of Long Island, which always included a casual, seafood lunch at Gosman's Dock. I usually ordered a clam chowder and a fried calamari platter that included fries. I sat with my parents at one of the white, plastic tables on the dock and while we ate we watched the fishing boats pulling in and out of the harbor, guessing what they might be bringing back to shore.

I remember riding into NYC on the train with my sister who took me to my first girls out lunch in Manhattan. I was 15, young and green and sitting inside a brasserie called The French Roast on the lower East Side, with different kinds of people. I ordered what my sister ordered, a burger with brie, a cheese I had never tasted before. I felt cool trying something new. I was growing up.

I remember my college graduation in Central Park and after the ceremony I got in the car and drove down the FDR Drive and over the Brooklyn Bridge to have lunch at the Hunter Steakhouse. I ate what I will always remember to be the best medium well-cooked Porterhouse steak, with a side of mashed potatoes, and then visited my elderly grandmother nearby who wanted to congratulate me as well.

I remember the morning I arrived in Rome for my new job and Marco, who I barely knew at the time, was at the airport waiting to take me to my apartment. Before we left, I had a cappuccino and a chocolate-filled *cornetto* from the airport café (I always loved them, told you) but I was too shy to eat it all in front of him. I asked for a small, paper bag and brought it home and then when he left that afternoon I ate the last bites.

I remember my wedding reception in the Roman countryside and all the food I didn't get to eat and enjoy. The menu included two first courses, a shrimp scampi risotto and ravioli with radicchio and smoked provola cheese, and a main course of braised beef in a red-wine Brunello di Montalcino sauce with baby potatoes and vegetables au gratin. I passed on all of this because I didn't have the stomach to eat. I did try a few bites of the vanilla and strawberry cream cake because I had too during the cake cutting ceremony, but I wish I could have eaten more.

I accept that in Germany a lot of my memories are going to be tied to eating in rather than eating out. I organized my daughter's seventh birthday party here and prepped everything, including a milk chocolate, triple layer birthday cake because we weren't fond of the store-bought ones we had ordered in the past. The cake I made nearly collapsed during the assembly part, and it could only be photographed from one side, but my daughter said it was "delicious" and that it was the "best cake ever." I was glowing and it wasn't even my birthday. Or the Easter Monday picnic I prepared on a rainy, cold day here in GK. In Italy, we often went out to eat on what the Italians call *Pasquetta* and enjoyed the fresh air and what marked the so-called beginning of Spring. I made a focaccia, zucchini pie, and mini meatballs, and we ate outside under the gazebo with coats and hats on because it was drizzling and cold. I think I do know now how to answer my GP. The best place to eat in GK is…at my home.

Not blinded by the light

I miss wearing sunglasses. I especially love the big, oversized, chunky frame ones because they make me feel sophisticated. No need for sunglasses, in GK though. The sky is mostly gray, there is lots of variety, but it's all in the same family — pastel gray, ash gray, slate gray.

I long for bright sun. I want its warmth on my face and body. I know that since I've been living in GK I've been missing out on all its advantages.[93] I'm definitely not getting the recommended 10 – 15 minutes of daily exposure needed to release serotonin that helps with my overall feelings of happiness. I'm not getting much support with my Vitamin D production, which helps my body absorb calcium and mineralize. I also could use some sunlight to regulate my internal clock, my Circadian rhythms. Instead, I take a daily cocktail of vitamins. On the other hand, I don't have to worry about the dangers of sun stroke or heat exhaustion. I don't think much about SPF protection. Dehydration is a non-issue here.

What preoccupies me here is the cold temperature, the rain, and the humidity. Beside my Podcasts app, the other most consistently used app on my phone is The Weather Channel. I check it first thing every morning, trying to answer the following questions: How cold is today? What coats should we wear? Are hats, scarves, and gloves necessary? Do we need wellies? In this part of Germany there is lots of *das Unwetter*, which means storm, but not a regular storm, a bad one, a severe one, an unusual one. The literal translation would be "unweather," which is a point the Germans are trying to make. The

---

[93]. Tansill-Suddath, Callie. "4 health benefits of sunlight and how much you should get each day." *Business Insider*, 7 Aug. 2020, insider.com/guides/health/mental-health/benefits-of-sunlight

weather is so bad that it's not even called weather anymore.

Like I mentioned, my fear of cold drafts began in Italy. I woke up one winter morning in Rome and couldn't move my head. I had pain and stiffness. I visited my doctor, who sent me for a neck X-ray, and then I was diagnosed with *la cervicale*, inflammation of the upper vertebrae, the ones that support the neck and the head. I had to see a physiotherapist for a few weeks, who put heat lamps on me and massaged my neck, but my doctor told me I would have to deal with this for the rest of my life. But now in GK, in Germany, *la cervicale* is worse. I know I need to get out of here before it becomes unbearable.

But hunkering down during the cold and/or rainy periods in GK isn't really possible. I would never leave the house. I couldn't do that. But surely there are limits. At the parents' orientation at my daughter's international school I heard one of the head teachers explain that the children would go outside at least twice a day, no matter the weather, rain or shine. What? They are going to let five-year-old kids play outside in the rain? I must have had that look of disapproval because the teacher looked directly at me and said, "there is no such thing as bad weather, just bad clothing." I left the school and realized that I needed to go shopping.

The jackets and coats, and suede or leather-heeled boots, that I brought from Rome didn't work in this part of Europe. I was acting as if I was in Italy; dressed for the season, but not the weather. I looked good but I had clothes that weren't warm enough and weren't water and wind resistant. I was often cold probably because my feet were getting wet all the time. I couldn't survive here with my fashionable, Italian gear.

I searched for waterproof, windproof, and breathable icons on the tags of jackets and shoes, something I never paid much attention to before. I kept looking for something decent, but the outdoor gear market is in its own design universe and the patented materials like Cordura and Coolmax sounded as if they should be worn by people who worked in the BASF chemical plant. I tried to buy a jacket from the big outdoorsy brands but I just couldn't do it. This New Yorker has never slept in a tent or owned a sleeping bag. I turned to the Italians again, this time to Northern Italians who understand the cold better. I settled on a long (to my knees) Italian down jacket that had the right combination of functionality and design. I was dry and warm, and I didn't look like an Eskimo, (no offense to the indigenous circumpolar peoples). I started to dress my kids in similar types of gear and was extra thrilled that their jackets and shoes even had reflectors on them — not only were they warm but they could be seen 350 meters away.

I did have the not-so brilliant idea of signing my daughter up for soccer on the NATO GK team. I thought it would be fun for her to play. I like girls who play soccer; they are strong and cool. I figured, though, that when it rained or when it was really cold, the practices and games would be canceled. But I was wrong. The Cheetah Dragons team practiced and played in all weather conditions. I was mortified. I skipped out on one or two practices, even an away game — there were torrential downpours — but I couldn't miss all of them, especially since my daughter kept begging me to go. And they were short of players: if one kid was missing, a position was often left uncovered. I prayed when she played in the rain. I worried she would get sick. I was also concerned about myself because I was the one standing on the side of the field watching her. I couldn't leave her unsupervised, but the chill, *la cervicale.*

The worst was during a cold, rainy, away game against a local German team in the nearby town of Birgden. These children, who had proper matching uniforms (our kids just wore the same color shirt), were organized and focused. They were passing and shooting, they even seemed to have a strategy. But when it started to rain hard and puddles began to form on the turf, the NATO kids stopped playing the game and focused on the rain. They jumped in the muddied puddles. They opened their mouths and tried to taste the rainwater. They were all over the place. They got crushed 14-1, and my daughter cried that it wasn't fair. I told myself that we were never doing this again, but after the season ended with a pizza party and trophies (Oh God, no!), my daughter kept asking me to play soccer again. I reluctantly signed her up again for the spring season, but it was more of the same, including the rain.

And while it was awfully unpleasant outside, our house in Waurichen just outside of GK center was perfect. The home was warm and cozy, its thermal envelope, you know everything that protects the living space from the outdoor elements, was ideally tight. It wasn't drafty, it had airtight doors and triple pane glass windows filled with krypton gas. The underfloor heating kept the house at our desired temperature of 22 degrees. You have to take your hat off to German engineering. As a matter of fact, I was actually warmer at home in GK during the fall and winter than I was in Italy.

Let me explain. Italian homes are basically ice boxes that seal in the cold, damp air. I always felt like it was colder indoors than outdoors. The houses and apartment buildings are made of cement laid over concrete slabs, and because many are old, historic structures, they haven't been updated when it comes to heating, ventilation, and air conditioning (HVAC). They don't pay much attention to insulation, weatherstripping, and caulking. The flooring is traditionally marble or tile and this feels cold to the touch, especially in the winter. I used to like to walk around barefoot on the squeaky, parquet wood floors in my childhood home, but in Italy I started to own slippers, multiple pairs, with thick plastic soles.

The other problem is that Italians have a different attitude when it comes to heating. I know that Italy has some of the highest electric and gas costs in the EU[94] but they don't follow the normal rule of setting your indoor thermostat to an ideal temperature and then letting the system work, with the heat coming on automatically if the house or apartment falls below the desired temperature. In Italy, they keep the heat off all day, then turn it on for a few hours in the evening and then off again. To my mind, they are wasting energy this way, surely the system has to work harder to warm up if it's turned completely off.

My mother-in-law's apartment in Naples is a 120-square-meter fridge. I've always dreaded going there in the fall and winter because it meant I would be cold for the duration of the visit, and that could be hours or even days. I never thought it was normal to see a fleeting, misty cloud (or what my kids call dragon breath) when I exhaled while

---

94. "Electricity Prices in Europe - Who Pays The Most?" Strom-Report, March 2021, strom-report.de/electricity-prices-europe/

sitting on her icy beige leather couch with a brown and orange plaid blanket covering my legs. I must admit that my mother-in-law has always made an effort while we were there, (I always found flannel zip-up robes and boot-like slippers for each of us) but her top-floor apartment is so poorly insulated — drafts of air from windows and doors — that it's never warm and comfortable. The only reprieve was when we got in the car and the heat was pumping but if we were going to visit my brother-in-law and his family nearby it only got worse. They rarely turned the heat on. They explained, while dressed in multiple layers that include sky-high turtlenecks and thick and loudly designed socks that the heat is "not really needed" and that they "warm up under the blankets at night." Then when I took off my coat, revealing my normal, non-arctic winter clothing, they would ask me in a patronizing way, "Aren't you cold?" I didn't want to be rude and so I always said, "No, I'm fine," but what I really wanted to yell at them was, "Of course I'm cold, there's no fricking heat on in here, and you keep opening the door to smoke and let the dog in and out. WTF." Later when my husband's brother and his family came to visit us in GK for a weekend in December, they found our warm, comfortable home to be too hot and stuffy. They complained and even asked to open up the windows in the dead of winter. I answered with an icy stare.

The outdoors in GK do get better in the spring and summer but that doesn't always mean warm or even hot. A jacket always has to be nearby. Fun and flirty sandals or open-toe shoes, barely get much use here. In New York I was able to wear sandals at least until late September. In Italy, I could wear them until October. In GK, I mostly see locals wearing orthopedic-like trekking sandals with socks. Yech. But just like in other places, the summer here also means pool parties and barbecues.

During our first summer in GK, I noticed a large advertisement posted near the main entrance for the base's annual August pool party. The base has an outdoor, heated Olympic-size swimming pool and a smaller kid's pool. I'm not a big pool person. I don't swim unless I have to, but I thought it would be nice to spend time outdoors and at least try, I said try, to meet new people. The day of the pool party was miserable. It was raining heavily, and the temperature dropped to 14 degrees Celsius. I figured it would be canceled, but it wasn't and so my husband said, "let's go anyway." I'd never been to a summer pool party wearing pants, a hooded jacket, and wellies. I found it strange but everyone else acted as if it was normal, drinking beer from the on-site truck and eating bratwurst.

The following summer when my mother-in-law visited we were experiencing a few warm days and so she wanted to get my daughter a kiddies' garden pool. I tried to explain to her that it probably wasn't the best investment because the warm weather wouldn't last. She insisted and asked my husband to take her out to buy one. I thought they would pick up one of those small, blue-clam-shaped pools that could easily be filled up with about 12 gallons of water, but she convinced my husband to buy an almost 100-gallon inflatable pool. I saw the box and thought, "they've completely lost it." My husband pulled out his small air compressor from the garage and began to fill the huge blue and orange pool, and then added all the water. The day was warm, not hot, and by the time it was all set up clouds started to hover above. Then after about 15 minutes of jumping and playing, my daughter said she was cold and wanted to get out. I could see that my mother-in-law wanted her to stay in and practically got in it herself to entice her to stay. That night it rained. It rained for the next seven days straight.

All this weather paranoia is why I often listen to *The Good News Podcast*, which is like a bit of sunshine on a cloudy or rainy day. The podcast's hosts, Colleen Pellissier and Neil Jacobson, describe the show as "your source for good news, fun stories, auditory delight and sonic joy," and the short, little episodes that average three to five minutes are exactly that. They make me think how great it is out there in the world even if the weather here is so sucky. In one episode, I learned about how nonprofits in Europe are helping empower the homeless[95] by training them as walking tour guides in cities like Amsterdam, Berlin, Dublin. What a great initiative.

---

95. Pellisser, Colleen, and Neil Jacobsen, hosts. "A New Kind of Walking Tour." *The Good News Podcast*, 27 Sept. 2019, thegoodnewspodcast.fm/episodes/a-new-kind-of-walking-tour

In another episode, the hosts talked about those huge, soft, floppy teddy bears,[96] that you can see in pubs, cafés, metro stations, balconies, all over the Les Gobelins neighborhood of Paris. The project, which came from a local bookshop owner, was about bringing the community together in a fun and unexpected kind of way. How sweet, that put a smile on my otherwise frozen winter face. Or in another episode, they talked about a positive initiative at West Side High School in Newark, New Jersey.[97] The principal noticed some students were being bullied for coming to school with dirty clothes, and so he opened up a laundromat on campus, where students could do a load of laundry for free after school. The initiative not only gives disadvantaged students confidence but also teaches them a life skill. That's just inspiring, we need more administrators and educators like that.

I especially connected with the episode in which the hosts shared some cold weather happiness tips[98] after a polar vortex hit Chicago, where the podcast is produced. I feel like this part of Germany is always in the middle of a large area of low-pressure and frigid air. They suggested working out, eating foods that can help with your mood, like whole grains, fruits, and veggies. And finally they said just try and be happy about dreary weather, "be positive, be excited." Woohoo! Try to see it more positively, like the Danes and Swedes. This, I thought, was hard, but I could at least try and be more open-minded.

I have tried to focus on the few positives. In the cold and damp, I don't suffer much from allergies anymore, the chill has suppressed most pollen levels at least during the colder months. I must say that

---

96. Pellisser, Colleen, and Neil Jacobsen, hosts. "The Whimsical Teddy Bears of Paris." *The Good News Podcast*, 6 Feb. 2019, thegoodnewspodcast.fm/episodes/the-whimsical-teddy-bears-of-paris

97. Pellisser, Colleen, and Neil Jacobsen, hosts. "Sudsy at School." *The Good News Podcast*, 31 Aug. 2018, thegoodnewspodcast.fm/episodes/sudsy-at-school

98. Pellisser, Colleen, and Neil Jacobsen, hosts. "Cold Weather Happiness Tips." *The Good News Podcast,* 4 Feb. 2019, thegoodnewspodcast.fm/episodes/cold-weather-happiness-tips

my skin does look pretty good, everyone thinks I'm younger than I actually am. I guess the cooler temperatures are constraining my blood vessels, making me less prone to redness and swelling and the lack of sun means that I'm not getting skin damage. And every once in a while, I wear sunglasses outdoors when it's cloudy, if I need a little bit of a pick-me-up. Just to make a statement.

Needed: verb form of LOL

There are days when my kids are out of control and driving me to near madness, and nothing seems to be going the way I want or need it to be. I know that this is when I really need to laugh and I need to do it in the high-emotional-arousal-kind-of way, you know where I'm crying and I feel like I'm going to pee myself. I need the laughter that releases endorphins, the feel-good chemicals. The experts all say laughing is good for us and that it has a lot (of other) benefits.[99] The short-term ones include stimulation of essential organs, like the heart and lungs, and soothing all our built-up tension. In the long term, laughter improves the immune system, relieves pain, increases personal satisfaction, and boosts our overall mood.

I know I am uptight with my expectations, routines, and schedules but I still like to laugh. And as you can tell, I really need some of those laughter benefits, especially in this rainy, serious place. The problem is that laughing in another country, in another culture, in a foreign place where the native language is not English is like doing a split, which for me is hard, basically impossible. I'm just not that flexible.

In Italy, I was a fluent speaker, had a strong, somewhat innate understanding of the culture and way of life, but even so I still had trouble getting Italian comedy. I tried to join Marco and watch or listen to Maurizio Battista, one of his favorite Roman stand-up comedians, but I just couldn't laugh. I didn't find what he was joking about (he often used news articles to segue into his routine) to be funny. I felt like I was in a haze, somewhat lost, out of place, meanwhile my husband was cracking up and getting all those benefits of laughter. I wanted to join in, I truly did, but all I could do was sit

---

99. "Healthy Lifestyle, Stress Management." *Mayo Clinic,* 29 July 2021, mayoclinic.org/healthy-lifestyle/stress-management/in-depth/stress-relief/art-20044456

there and produce one of those tight, forced smiles.

I also sat through countless *cinepannetoni*, a particular genre of Italian film released around Christmas each year, which use an exaggerated type of comedy. The films usually include a holiday trip where the characters meet other Italians, things go horribly wrong, but in the end they all reconcile. I sat in the cinema surrounded by dozens of people who were all laughing out loud but again it wasn't funny to me. I always felt like an outsider and the whole experience was weird, even somewhat creepy. In Germany, I didn't even understand the language or the culture to help me laugh at their comedy. I wouldn't even know where or how to find it, and I never cared enough to look because we were just passing through. I also assumed that the well-known stereotypes that Germans were humorless and didn't understand irony were true. I knew the supposed line from Mark Twain, "A German joke is no laughing matter."

Luckily, I found that podcasts could also lighten the load when I needed a pick me up, when I felt the urge to escape a bit and laugh in English. I searched through a lot of podcasts labeled as comedy, with stand-up filling up much of that space — it does seem like every comedian or celebrity has their own podcast now. I listened to a variety of them, including a few episodes of *Katherine Ryan: Telling Everybody Everything* podcast. I had read about Ryan, a Canadian expat based in London, and her success. The episodes of her show were like one big extended monologue in which she mused about life and big topics like miscarriages, showbiz sexism, racism, cancel culture. I know that comedy can shine a light on these issues, but it was challenging for me to find humor in episodes about climate change or racism.

I also listened to some episodes of the *Entry Level with Brooks Wheelan* podcast, in which Wheelan, a former cast member on Saturday Night Live (SNL), America's late-night comedy skit show that has been around since 1975, talked to guests about a low-paying job they had before they obtained success in the entertainment industry. I moved to the funky, intro music with the chorus "your entry level" and learned a lot about how some celebrities had to work their way up the ladder. But was the podcast making me laugh? No, not happening. I also downloaded a so-called humorous storytelling series like *This is Branchburg,* which is made up of a mix of sketches, monologues, and character studies about the bizarre residents of Branchburg, a fictionalized version of Branchburg, a real town in New Jersey. I couldn't get into the escapist plot and the darkly absurd take on the trivial aspects of life. I wasn't laughing.

I wanted entertainment made up of jokes, satirical sketches, and storytelling that I could relate to, that I could identify with personally. I need a connection in order to laugh, to chuckle a bit. I need to feel like I've been there or that I know what that comedian is talking about first-hand. I need to have shared the experience in some way, even minimally, and that's why I began to find *The Pete and Sebastian Show* podcast hit home with me. The weekly podcast hosted by Pete Correale and Sebastian Maniscalco is one big rambling conversation between the two stand-up comedians. They catch up with what's been going on in their lives, including dealing with people, such as family and friends, disciplining their children, and figuring out how things actually work. This is not a smart, high-brow comedy. In fact, it's more like the raw, bad grammar, "yo, bro," ridiculous kind. Correale is from Oakdale, a town on Long Island just miles from where I spent part of my childhood, and Maniscalco, who is from Chicago, is the son of Italian immigrants.

Like Maniscalco, I know that being first-generation Italian American means doing a lot of things for your parents. He often talks about his family's work ethic and how his father told him to start a business at eight years old. I didn't have to become a limited liability corporation, but I did have to help my parents with a lot of everyday things, and it wasn't because they didn't know how to do them. There just came a time when they started relying exclusively on their native English-speaking children because it was easier. I was a guru at making appointments and getting referrals for doctors or medical exams. I learned the tricks (*si, habla español* or yes, I am using a rotary phone, I'll hang on) to bypass the automatic messaging and get straight to a person who could help. I pretended to be my mother, and I often heard comments that I had such a "young voice" for someone born in 1947. I lied, but my mother said, "every so often a little lie is necessary," especially if it was to help the family.

135

I was also pretty good at managing their money. Once I could handle somewhat complex math, which was at about sixth grade, I was overseeing their checking account. I thought back then it was because my mother knew how much I liked playing bank. On one Saturday morning each month she handed me a stack of mail to go through. I was so excited when we got a gold letter opener as a party favor for a family wedding. I made sure the bills and invoices were valid and then wrote checks to all the payees. I gave them to my mother to approve and sign, kind of like the way an office manager does for the head of a company but without the black-leather, embossed signing pad. I also wrote all our holiday cards because my mother said it was good for me to practice my cursive handwriting. I did always have my mother actively supervising me, especially when I was on the phone, she would be mouthing words and gesticulating the points she wanted me to make. Later, when I started driving, which I probably delayed subconsciously because I knew what would happen (I was 20 years old), I had to run all sorts of errands. I picked up prescriptions from the pharmacy, Italian bread from the bakery, took in my mother's car for an oil change and tire rotation, and even drove her and her friends around. I once brought a car full of Italian ladies into Queens for an all-day Lenten retreat because after years of living in the suburbs my mother said she no longer felt "comfortable" driving in the city traffic.

My father also expected help. He owned his own auto body collision repair shop and had a dealer's license that allowed him to purchase cars that were declared "total loss," which meant the cost of making repairs exceeded the actual cash value of the car. He would buy cars that had been in accidents from auctions, fix them, and sell them. I got my first car this way, $600 for a 1993, red, Ford Taurus. I named her Susy. I was always so proud of my father, an Italian immigrant who by himself opened his own successful business and supported not only his wife and children but also for many years his mother, his sister, his brother, and even his brother-in-law. I slowly and oddly became responsible for all the dealership's paperwork that my father had previously handled on his own. When he came home from work with his brown, hard-sided attaché case covered with dust and splattered with auto paint, I knew there was paperwork that I needed to fill out (otherwise he left the briefcase in the office at his shop).

Interestingly, most of the helping was delegated to my sister and me, while our two older brothers were barely asked to do anything. I didn't think it was because they were boys and we were girls, there was no gender inequality in our home, but I felt my parents thought we were a bit more paper-work capable. I reveled in that feeling. I can remember my mother often saying that if she had four daughters, instead of just two, she would be the richest woman in the world. I never talked about all the secretarial work I did to my American friends. They would find it weird that I pretended to be my mother on the phone and spent Saturday mornings writing checks, but to me it was part of what I had to do. Maniscalco's comedy podcast reminded me of all this.

I also had to help my parents fit into American life, assimilate to certain situations. I took a day off from work at my journalism job in my mid-20s to bring my mother into Manhattan to get her passport renewed at the Italian Consulate. She is a resident alien, which sounds out of this world, but what it meant was that she could live and work in the U.S. without renouncing her Italian citizenship. My mother loves America, New York, but never had any interest in becoming a U.S. citizen like some of our other family members.

I knew my mother had lived in New York longer than I was alive, but she still acted like a small-town girl from southern Italy. She's unsuspecting, sweet, and kind. She almost always has a smile on her face. She cares about other people and gives more than she takes. She is like a fairy godmother. She's the type of person that if someone says "I love that crochet scarf you have on..." she goes home, makes a similar one, and mails it all to them. (And this happens a lot because her crochet work is top-notch.) But my mother is not street smart, not a person who could handle large crowds and confusion. She is a bit naïve, she could easily get distracted by a cute baby and get her wallet or entire handbag stolen on the subway. I began to give her clear instructions a few days before our passport trip to Manhattan. I told her firmly that there was no smiling at children or adults, that she had to keep a straight, serious face, there would be no picking up trash, we weren't on a church mission, and that she needed to follow my lead and move along quickly. I knew it was hard for her to act this way, cold, without-a-heart, but I couldn't risk her sweet, unassimilated ways turning us into targets. She was, after all those years, a stranger in a strange land. As was I in Germany.

I'm sure if my kids were old enough, they would have yelled at me for participating in the local festivals dressed in regular, plain clothes — talk about not fitting in. In the Fall of our first year, we bought tickets to the GK base's Oktoberfest. The two-day event is a big affair and is even open to the public if you can find a sponsor who is a NATO ID holder We planned to meet up with a few other Italian families also stationed at GK, and everyone agreed that they weren't going to wear the traditional Bavarian attire. I had seen dirndl and lederhosen for sale in some of the local shops, but I thought, "there's no way we're going to embarrass ourselves and wear this stuff." That night we passed through the security check, walked into the blue-and-white decorated hangar where the festivities were happening and noticed that of the about 3,000 people present, we were part of the group of about 15 Italians and one American (me) who decided to wear jeans and sweaters instead of the traditional clothing. We were the freaks, the weirdos, who looked like we didn't belong. I was red in the face, and it wasn't from the half liter artisanal beer I chugged quickly. I also had to deal with my daughter who kept asking me repeatedly, "Mommy, why don't I have a dress like that girl." I wanted to go home. The following year I dressed everyone up, including my then one-year-old son.

I also now have kids that are into local festivities. One day in early November my daughter came off the school bus with a hand-colored, paper lantern and begged me to participate in the St. Martin procession. I didn't know anything about St. Martin, except for the flier I had found in our mailbox that talked about an event on the 11 November with a 7:00 p.m. start time at the *Feuerhaus*, which was right across the street from our home. I agreed reluctantly. I secretly hoped the procession would be canceled because it was cold and drizzling. I was also a bit irritated. I couldn't understand why of all the saints that exist, the Germans had to make a big deal about St. Martin and his November feast? I mean couldn't they celebrate St. Thomas the Apostle, whose feast day is on 3 July, or St. Rose of Lima, who is celebrated 23 August. They are also great, virtuous saints and it would be nicer to celebrate when the days were long and weather was milder. Right?

The weather, however, was irrelevant to the locals because I could hear the *rabbimel, rabammel, rabumm* from the drums inside our home. I bundled us up and after a few minutes of waiting, St. Martin, dressed like a Roman soldier complete with a red cloak, arrived on a white horse, which I think belonged to our neighbor. St. Martin led the procession with the children and their lanterns, along with their parents, around the village, which included singing songs that my daughter had learned at school. She kept saying, "Sing, mommy, sing," and I hummed a bunch of nothing. The procession ended at the village's public square where there was a giant bonfire, which looked wild, made for TV, even a bit dangerous, but the firefighters looked ready if anything got out of hand. The locals each picked up a type of sweet bread that was shaped like a man with raisin eyes and a white, nonedible pipe. I didn't have tickets for the bread, I didn't know about the breadman. I probably should have translated the flier. So, at the following year's St. Martin's procession I carried a piece of paper with all the popular St. Martin songs so I could sing along (although it was dark out and hard to read). I ordered four breadmen, way too much. I even added my own touch to the breadman when we got home — I sliced through him and spread on a thick layer of hazelnut cream. Who says I'm not adaptable?

I also realized how hard it must have been for my mother when my siblings and I expected to celebrate American holidays. I'm sure it was strange for her at first to buy costumes and dress us up like our favorite characters for Halloween, but she did anyway. I suppose it was different to make corned beef and boiled cabbage for St. Patrick's Day, the traditional meal in the U.S., but she kept with local tradition. She did, though, always make her mother's, my *nonna's*, plain, good-for-dunking-in-milk cookies for every holiday, but instead of them being shaped like Ss, she made pumpkins for Halloween and four-leaf clovers with green sprinkles for St. Patrick's Day.

The Pete and Sebastian Show comedy podcast also uses part of its hour-long episodes, which I often need to listen to in two or three different moments, talking about doing and trying new things. For example, when Pete changed the tires on his camper or when he checked into a hotel where there was no reception — a bit complicated. Or when Sebastian pulled out his new power washer and went cologne shopping — not so simple. I thought about the gadgets my family sends me and how sometimes things go terribly wrong. They know I want to stay in the loop, be in-the-know even though I live overseas in a tiny village, and therefore whenever something fun or useful hits the market, whether it's big or small, I get a care package. The package always includes some type of clothing for my kids and my husband, along with an airtight container filled with mother's homemade cookies. She always makes cherry filled almond-paste cookies and olive oil cookies with homemade jam. She's a perfectionist, which means every cookie is the same size and shape, and they look as amazing as they taste.

Finally, there is a small gadget that's just hit the market in the US. The stuff eventually makes its way for sale here and globally, but at least I think I get it first, which makes me feel kind of cool. I once got a small, battery-operated tabletop crumb sweeper that looked like a red beetle, which is good for picking up crumbs in those hard to clean crevices. My son liked it so much he got his index finger stuck in the small hole on the bottom, and we had to rub him with olive oil to get it out. I also received a musical birthday candle that starts with a shower of sparks that shoot upward, before petals open like a blooming flower, and all of the mini candles on each of the petals light up. It then starts rotating and playing happy birthday. I'm sure this was illegal to ship via international mail. I used the candle for my birthday and it did all of those things — sparks upward, candle petals opened, but when the candles started rotating, the frilly purple pom poms that decorated my vanilla custard cream cake with whip cream frosting caught fire and so did the candle's accouterments. I froze a bit and watched it start to burn, my kids looked at the cake in fear, with their hands partially covering their eyes, and my husband continued singing until he realized that the fire was starting to grow and spread. He finally reacted by picking up the candle and the pom poms and throwing them in the kitchen sink. The music faded into a dark, unrecognizable tune before it stopped.

For quick-and-easy laughs I listen to the *Netflix Is A Daily Joke* podcast that features short soundbites from stand-up comedy specials. The content is easy, snackable, most episodes are under five minutes, and help me to stop taking myself too seriously and laugh at my life. I know Netflix wants me to go and watch the full special on demand, but these bits are usually enough for me. In the episode that included a few minutes from Steve Martin and Martin Short's special called "An Evening You Will Forget For the Rest of Your Life,"[100] the old-school comedians laughed at the pale, white color of Steve Martin's skin. Short described him like a clean page in a coloring book and even said that Martin once got a sunburn from his Kindle reader.

The joke got me thinking about how Italians, in particular my husband's tan family, have always reacted to my skin color. As I said already, I like (and now miss) the sun, but not enough according to Italian standards.

Italians adore the sun in the same kind of way the Ancient Greeks worshiped the god Helios, minus the prayers. They use a lot of sun-related words to describe people positively. The word *solare* is used to characterize someone who is radiant, cheerful, and sunny, meanwhile a young woman who is beautiful is called *bella come il sole*. Italians are basically tanorexics and feel that everyone must bask in the sun whenever possible, especially throughout the summer months. I understand, the country has about 5,000 miles of coastline with awe-inspiring beaches and they should be enjoyed, but the fact that I didn't have a deep, dark tan by the time August or early September arrived was unfathomable to them. I was judged, they looked at me as if something was wrong, like there was a defect in my DNA. Each year, as soon as I wore short sleeves or a skirt without tights, they commented that I was "so white" and it was followed by, "Do you not like the beach and the sun?" I always answered, "Yes, I do." I guess they didn't remember that I did enjoy the beach and that Long Island is surrounded by water and has some lovely white sand beaches on the East Coast, including the world-famous Jones Beach and East

---

100. Short, Martin, and Steven Martin, narrators. "Some Jokes about Hollywood Compliments." *Netflix is a Daily Joke*, 30 April 2020, netflix-is-a-daily-joke.simplecast.com/episodes/steve-martin-and-martin-short-some-jokes-about-hollywood-compliments-JibcZHzM

Hampton Main Beach.

Now it wasn't as if I walked around with a parasol or stayed in cool, shady places all day. I'm just fair skinned. I'm not whole milk white but to help you understand I use the lightest color of concealer and foundation, on a scale from one to five, with one being the lightest color, I'm always one. I have the kind of skin that burns, that becomes red, hot, and itchy when it's first exposed to the sun and then after a few more days at the beach I start to get what I consider to be a healthy, sun-kissed light golden look, but not deep, dark color. I was always happy with it but to Italians this was unacceptable, symbolic of someone who didn't spend enough time at the beach and therefore didn't enjoy the sun.

In this one thing I fit in better in Germany. Here I'm not the only pale face. I look, at least from a skin-tone perspective, as if I blend in with the crowd. The locals live a lot of their days without the sun, and many have fair complexions all year round, even in the summer months (along with beautiful, naturally blond hair, not highlighted like mine). I didn't feel like I needed to buy self-tanning lotions, which I tried only once in Italy — the streaking, my God, never again. I'm not embarrassed walking around in the early Spring with arms and legs that haven't seen the light of day in a year. I don't feel like I'm being mocked or stared at because I don't have a tan. That's me — pale and proud.

But my stature, my physical size, is a completely different story. The women here are big and tall and tower over me. In a ranking of the 25 countries with the tallest people,[101] Germany is listed at number 14 with an average height of about 172 cm, or 5 feet, 8 inches for men. The average German woman is 165 cm, or 5 feet, 5 inches tall. Italy and the United States don't even make the list. I'm 158 cm, or 5 feet, 2 inches tall, a peanut, a shrimp in comparison to most of my neighbors. I feel it here especially when I go to the hair salon; in order to do my hair my stylist needs to pump the chair up all the way.

---

101. Bostock, Bill. "Ranked: The countries with the tallest people in the world." *Business Insider*, 26 June 2019, www.insider.com/tallest-people-world-countries-ranked-2019-6

I look like my daughter when she's getting a haircut but unlike her, I don't swing my legs back and forth.

It's true that from a human anatomy perspective, taller people usually have bigger feet, but both my sister and I were taken aback the first time we went into a German shoe store. It was my first summer in GK and my sister had flown in from New York to help me get settled, which included checking out the area and some of its shops. I vividly remember that we looked at each other with that mouth-open, holy shit, (yeah, I cursed,) can-you-believe-this-face because we had never seen such big shoes before. We touched, caressed them, picked them up, turned them upside down, to make sure they were real. They reminded me of those funny shoes people try on or get in when they're at an amusement park, country fair, or some place in the Netherlands, you know, ha-ha, big clogs. In the U.S. and Italy, the display shoe for women is usually a 36 or 37 (that's 6 or 7 U.S. size) but in GK they were showing sizes 41 and 42 (11 and 12). I could fit at least two of my size 36 feet into one of these shoes.

The Netflix comedy podcast also made me realize how bad and ridiculous my German language skills were after I listened to Anjelah Johnson's joke from her comedy special "Not Fancy" about learning Spanish.[102] She explained that because of her Mexican origins people assume she speaks Spanish and start chatting away at her. She goes along and at the end of the conversation she uses a go-to Spanish phrase like *ai, que bueno*, or *klaro, que si* but most of the time it has nothing to do with the conversation.

I'm grasping with laughter because I do that too. I try to act like I speak German, like I'm one of those fascinating trilingual people. I don't want to admit that I only know key words in German, in particular the ones that sound like English words. I want to try to speak and so when I go places, say, a doctor's appointment, I walk in and I say to the receptionist slowly *Ich habe einen Termin* (translation: I have an appointment). But then they usually rattle something else off

---

102. Johnson, Annjelah, narrator. "A Joke About Learning Spanish." *Netflix is a Daily Joke,* 4 May 2020, netflix-is-a-daily-joke.simplecast.com/episodes/annjelah-johnson-a-joke-about-learning-spanish-blor3BNg

quickly and if it's not take a *sitz* over there or can I have your insurance *Karte* I'm lost. I then start speaking English and apologize for not speaking German. I feel bad about it.

The most ridiculous thing, according to my husband, is when the doorbell rings and I answer through the intercom system as if I understand. The back and forth often goes like this:

Me: *Hallo!*

Them: asds jfjshjvn xfjdhfksdj paket

(To myself: I understood package.)

Me: *Danke!*

I then hang up and get back to what I was doing. I don't have to get the package right away, nobody steals anything here in quietville. But sometimes less than a minute later there is another ding dong.

Them: asds jfjshjvn xfjdhfksdj paket

(To myself: I don't understand. I had better open the door)

Them: fsdldfjdslkfsk fjdslfjdks djsadksladj with hand gesture showing that a signature is required for the delivery of the package.

Me: *Ja, danke; ja, ja danke, danke!*

I even had a revelation of sorts about the Italian wives in GK thanks to the *Netflix is a Daily Joke* podcast. In Ali Wong's special called "Baby Cobra" she chatted about housewives[103] and the resentment towards them. She mentioned former Facebook CEO Sheryl Sandberg's bestselling book *Lean in: Women, Work and the Will to Lead* that encouraged women to push themselves forward, voice their opinions, and work towards gender equality. But Wong said, "I don't want to lean in, okay, I want to lie down. I want to lie the fuck down." I'm laughing, my stomach hurts. She said feminism was the worst thing to happen to women and that it was better when "our job, was no job." She added that women had it good and that they

---

103. Wong, Ali, narrator. "A Joke about Housewives." *Netflix is a Daily Joke*, 18 May 2020, netflix-is-a-daily-joke.simplecast.com/episodes/ali-wong-a-joke-about-housewives-ZkY1fHd2

should have done the smart thing, which would have been to continue to play dumb for the next century. Wong said women get upset at her comments and believe they do have "so many more options now," but she said that "women had a lot more options when their days were free, unscheduled, unsupervised, and most importantly sponsored."

I had tended to look at the Italian wives in a judgmental kind of way, which I know wasn't very nice of me. I was annoyed by them because I thought they were too submissive to their husbands as if they lived their daily lives according to the Bible. I've always cringed a bit at that passage from Ephesians 5:22 – 33 that instructs wives to submit to their husbands, as they would the Lord. Every so often I heard it at Sunday mass (not all priests would quote this phrase, but some conservatives still do). It was even one of the readings the priest suggested for my nuptial mass. I immediately passed on it. I chose another reading from Genesis 2:18-24 about two becoming one body.

Over time I learned that for the most part the Italian wives at GK are not super religious. I wondered if they acted this way because they didn't have jobs. I thought if they worked, they could demand some more respect. I didn't think it was right that their husbands were driving around the GK base with expensive new cars like the Audi A5 Sport or a BMW X4 and they were driving beat-up utilitarian vehicles like the Fiat Punto. That's not fair. I wanted to wake them up a bit, help them see how they were being treated.

In a casual conversation with Graziella, an Italian wife from Latina, I learned that she woke up with her husband at 5:30 a.m. to make him coffee in the Moka pot before he left for work. I was a bit nauseated. I only asked why she was getting up with him. I thought all this: I might be mean, selfish, and a bad wife to my Italian husband, but I think he can make his own coffee. The Moka pot, who uses one? I thought everyone had some type of semi-automatic coffee machine in which you pop in a pod or capsule and then push a button. And how about a better idea, why doesn't your husband just buy a cup of coffee on-the-go, it's 5:30 in the frickin morning. Graziella said she just wanted to help her husband. I was silent.

But thanks to Ali Wong, I figured it out. Here's my theory: When

Graziella sent her husband off at 5:30 a.m. and got her kids to school, she was free, she did what she wanted, which probably included going back to bed, waking up whenever she felt like it, and then eating whatever and whenever she wanted without anyone bothering her. I get it, the Italian wives are not dumb. They act compliant and accommodating but they do whatever they want all day and get taken care of by their husbands without having any of the responsibilities that come along with keeping a job. I understood how smart they are, acting all submissive, when they basically run their own show for most of the day. Laughing out loud, funny, right?

Productively isolating

I didn't have much trouble adjusting to the solitary life of lockdown during Covid. I think it's because my life in Germany has been so different. I was used to being home, a lot, and that's why the actual lockdown, being stuck-inside part, wasn't difficult. I already lived somewhat in isolation.

I didn't, though, have a blissfully empty calendar. I was busy, really busy. I always had some work or parental activity going on. I was especially occupied with my kids. Like everyone else in lockdown, I was with them all day, every day for weeks, which then turned into months. I found that they had settled in relatively well to their new homebound life, but they were more needy than ever, always asking for something — a cup of juice, a hard-to-reach toy, help with the remote control. I was also stressing about our imminent departure, or PCSing as they call it in the military, because my husband's four-year assignment was coming to end, and of course Covid, getting sick or worse dying from the virus.

I tossed and turned most nights thinking about everything, especially Covid, wondering how scared I should actually be. I needed information and there were many new pop-up coronavirus podcasts that could give me data, analysis, and some know-how without more hype and hysteria. I was already in a panic. I took a break from some of my favorite podcasts, and I added some Covid information shows to my daily listening. I also, out of dire personal need, included a few other different podcasts to my library during my isolation.

The U.S. news organizations that I usually relied on were too narrow in scope. I tried to listen to *NPR's Consider This* (once called *Coronavirus Daily*), a podcast covering the pandemic, but it was mainly U.S. focused, and it was also behind the game for someone like me in Europe where we were a few weeks ahead in the spread of the virus.

I already knew how important it was to wash my hands for 20 seconds, not to touch my eyes, nose, and mouth, and how to grocery shop safely. I got more of the same from the *ABC News Radio Specials* podcast in its coverage of Covid-19. I couldn't, though, find an English language news podcast specific to Germany. I used *Der Spiegel* and *Die Zeit* websites for news in English, but they didn't have an English language podcast. I also relied on the news website *The Local Germany* for updates, but they also didn't offer additional content in the podcast form.

I was frustrated. I was mad at myself for not learning German. I had lived in Germany for more than three years and I was stuck using translation software for news stories. I even used an interpreter application to piece together former Chancellor Angela Merkel's live updates to residents — exhausting. I tried to learn German. I signed up for an elementary course on the GK base, just a few months after I arrived. I didn't want to become a polyglot; I just wanted some basic skills. The class was filled with Italians, some active military, but mostly wives, there were also a few Spaniards, a Pole, but no Americans. I didn't understand why at first, but I quickly learned that many of my classmates also didn't speak English, and therefore they had serious trouble communicating everywhere. Aside from the different nationalities, the GK base was like a small rural American town, almost everyone spoke English. Outside the base, I had found doctors who spoke English. I also used English at the supermarket and other shops if needed; there was always someone who understood. I attended German language classes for about three weeks but after my instructor made a comment about my American accent I was done with it. I stopped going. I don't usually give up, but it was the perfect excuse. I was unmotivated because I was getting along fine with just my English.

Covid-19, however, made me feel even more afraid and anxious than I normally am. I wanted and needed to understand news and information, without the help of some software program. I had read about how podcasts were also being used as a language tool, and so I dedicated some of my lockdown time to try podcasts such as *Easy German* and *GermanPod101.com* before deciding on *Coffee Break German*. I liked its simple instruction manner and the extensive repetition of words and phrases. I started with the basics, and I took it more seriously this time. I didn't do a full immersion — I couldn't with everything going on at home — but I listened regularly to two 20-minute episodes a week. I usually listened/studied during my son's nap time.

I relied a lot on *BBC World Service's Coronavirus Global Update* podcast because it offered me a complete view of what was going on in the world. The episodes were only about five minutes each, and during the height of the pandemic they aired two episodes per day. There was no consistency or familiarity when it came to the host as there were several reporters/producers whose voices led the show, but the update was all encompassing.

Before isolation, I might have accessed this type of news update from television, everyone turns to television in times of crisis,[104] but with my kids home their monopoly over the living room television quickly turned into sole ownership. If I interrupted their television time and watched the news, the noise level suddenly escalated. They would sing or play with toys that barked, beeped, or had a blaring siren and I had trouble hearing. I had to pause, go back, and listen again, it was cumbersome. I couldn't just leave my kids and go into another room. I wanted to sometimes, but I had to keep an eye on them. I often listened with just one earbud so that I could get the info I needed and still hear what they were up to.

I also added *CNN's Chasing Life* podcast (at the time called *Coronavirus: Fact or Fiction*) hosted by Chief Medical Correspondent Sanjay Gupta to my library. Gupta, a doctor whose face I knew from *CNN*, provided information and even some medical advice in a friendly, not alarming way.

The 10-minute episode about talking to kids about the coronavirus included an interview with *CNN* anchor and mother of two, Kate Bolduan. Bolduan said she first tried to protect her kids from the news, telling them that there was "nothing to worry about." I used that strategy at first too, especially since out of precaution and fear I

---

104. Jones, Katie. "How COVID-19 Has Impacted Media Consumption, by Generation." *Visual Capitalist*, 7 April 2020, visualcapitalist.com/media-consumption-covid-19/

pulled my daughter out of her school two weeks before it officially closed. My daughter: Is my school open this week? Why am I home? Me: Yes, it's open, but I wanted to keep you home so we could play and spend time together. Lie. I kept my daughter home because I heard and saw what was happening in Italy — the spread of the virus, the overwhelmed health care system, and the rising death toll. I acted as if I was in Italy. I did what the Italian government instructed its residents to do even though I was in Germany. The GK Base follows its own NATO guidelines, but it does take into consideration the host nation's rules, in this case Germany, which at first was slow to close things down. Meanwhile, the Netherlands, with its long liberal tradition, where my daughter's school was located, acted as if the virus didn't exist.

I doubted the theory that Italy was hit hard because of its poor healthcare system. Tourism is one of Italy's main industries. Before Covid-19, tourism represented 12 percent of the country's GDP (gross domestic product),[105] which means that there are tourists in Italy all year long, not only during the summer months. Yes, there are people who visit Stockholm and Copenhagen, but their numbers don't even come close to Italy's incoming traffic. I knew it was only a matter of time before the virus became a problem here and everywhere. But when the virus progressed *CNN's* Bolduan turned to the experts — pediatricians and psychologists — and they said children need reassurance in times of uncertainty and that it was important to "demystify the terms."

The experts also suggested "checking yourself" because kids pick up on what their parents are saying. How was I behaving? What was I saying on the phone to my mother? What conversations were my husband and I having at dinner? I was obviously scared and freaking out, which wasn't good. I didn't have to worry about my son, he was too small. I needed, though, to talk to my daughter. I had to explain to her what was really going on. She had questions, lots of them. She asked me where the virus came from. I told her it started in China

---

105. OECD. *Tourism Trends and Policies 2018*, Italy. OECD Publishing, Paris, doi.org/10.1787/tour-2018-24-en.

and then she called it the "virus from China." I knew that was bad, really bad, after the rise of anti-Chinese sentiment, and especially after former U.S. President Donald Trump repeatedly called it the "China virus" during news conferences, ignoring criticism that this was racist.

My daughter also asked me if it was in our small village, and I told her "no," because from my scrappy translations I had deduced that there weren't any cases here, at least at the time. My daughter thought the virus was in another part of Germany, far, far away from us. Little did she know that Gangelt, later known as "Germany's Wuhan," in the Heinsberg district of North Rhine-Westphalia, is where the country's first coronavirus case was confirmed, and it was just 15 km from our home. Gangelt is even closer to the GK base, and many military families live in the small town. Later during one of many walks around the neighborhood, the only outdoor activity we could do, my daughter asked to stop at the playground, but when she saw the yellow and black barrier tape on the merry-go-round, seesaw, and super slide she got upset and said, "I hate the virus from China. I hate it." She was little and only understood so much. At night when we prayed, my daughter asked God to "kill the virus" and "please kill it before my birthday so I can have a party with my friends." I urged her to imagine God as a gentle being, not some violent higher power, who destroyed things. I silently prayed for that too, I did.

To keep our days in isolation well balanced, I set up a schedule just like Astronaut Scott Kelly recommended in another episode of *Chasing Life*.[106] The veteran of four space flights, including one in which he commanded the International Space Station, said an organized day with time allotted for work, meals, and exercise was essential in confined situations. He spent an entire year in space.

The problem was that our days started way too early. I think we were the only family up at 6:30 a.m. with no place to go. I'm a morning person. I don't sleep until 10:00 or 11:00 a.m., but 7:30 a.m. would've been great during isolation, especially because I was so restless during the early morning hours. My son was an early riser and

---

106. Gupta, Sanjay, host. "Astronaut Scott Kelly on How to Survive Isolation." *Chasing Life*, 3 April 2020, globalplayer.com/podcasts/episodes/7Drb6Km/.

once he was up my daughter was up. "Mommy?," she would say. I stopped and waited for her — "put your socks on, go pee-pee, wash your hands" — and we'd all go down together and start the day. I often left my husband in bed with his eye mask on and as soon as we were gone, he put his yellow shooting earplugs in too. I knew our friends and family were sleeping in late because I wrote them messages and they wouldn't read and respond to them until at least 9:00 a.m. in whatever time zone they were in. I wasn't stalking them, but I could tell.

The weekdays began with work and cleaning and cooking in between. I also had my son hanging around, mostly pulling on my leg saying all the new words he was learning during isolation. The international school my daughter attended had been great — I was happy with the curriculum and her progress. She was enrolled in the British section, which offered full-time instruction in English. We chose the British section over the American section, because not only was it cheaper but we lived in Europe and thought it would be best for her (even if she was little) to learn some European culture and history. But when we began homeschooling, I started to feel overwhelmed. The week she had to learn how to tell time was exhausting. I figured clocks and time would be easier compared to the fractions work from the week prior, but it wasn't.

The British elementary school curriculum is quite advanced compared to the American one. I watched an online tutorial and learned that the fundamental skills to tell time were being able to count to 60, she could do that, and being able to count by fives, she could do that too. She was, however, clueless about what time she woke up and what time she ate lunch — "No, it's not at 3:00 p.m., come on!" I tried to break it down slowly for her and by the end of the week she could tell time and was even using the "quarter past" and "quarter to" terminology (as required by her teacher), but a few days later when I asked her what time it was, she was confused again. Was it possible for kids to forget things so easily? I blew up and was upset. I yelled and told her she wasn't listening. I made her cry. I felt bad but I clearly wasn't cut out for homeschooling. I couldn't understand families that homeschooled during non-pandemic times. I knew a few of them in GK, and I was now sure they were the most patient people ever.

The schedule also included, at least at the beginning of isolation, physical education (PE) with my daughter's class, which was also considered a must-do by astronaut Kelly. I received an email from her teacher to meet up online and exercise with Joe Wickes on YouTube. I assumed Joe Wickes was a PE teacher at her school, and that he was doing a special workout for the elementary students. I even asked my daughter about him, prying about whether he was a substitute when Coach Smith, the PE teacher I knew, wasn't there. "I don't know him," she said. Then when we signed in and I learned that Joe Wickes is a popular British health and fitness expert. He's basically a younger, British version of Richard Simmons or Jack LaLanne. I started exercising too, and while it wasn't a disciplined thing, at least I was moving my body a little.

Before the coronavirus, I had committed to a serious exercise regime. I was lucky because for my entire life I had eaten whatever I wanted without worrying about my weight. I only gained about 10 kilos during each of my pregnancies and lost the weight quickly without even breastfeeding or doing any kind of exercise. But when I turned 40, I started to see that being skinny was not enough because everything started to look un-toned and even feel somewhat softer, ugh. I hoped it was the fault of that mirror I bought on sale, but I knew it wasn't. I had to do something and started attending spinning class on the base. The class wasn't SoulCycle, no dim, candlelit studio, but it was high intensity cycling with loud, fast-paced music.

I showed up to my first class just minutes before it was about to start, not the smartest thing, and I quickly jumped on a free bike trying to act cool and fit in. I could barely touch the pedals because the seat was too high, and the handlebars were so far away that I was stretched out on top of the bike. It was uncomfortable and definitely unsustainable for the duration of the hour-long class. I must have looked ridiculous because a tall, already sweaty cyclist came to help. I thought, "How can he be so sweaty? The class hasn't even started, they were just warming up. Oh God!" I was slightly embarrassed, but thankful for the help. I figured the parts of the bike that I needed to adjust and turned into a regular. I sweated a lot too and it felt as if I was expelling toxins from my body. I know, a bit dramatic. I started to see results in just a few weeks. But as you might have imagined, the gym facilities on the GK base were one of the first things to close as the virus spread, and there went my exercise.

I quickly became more sedentary, less physically active, but I was cooking and eating a lot more. I was doing it the Italian way. I didn't make sandwiches for lunch anymore, but instead I prepared vegetables and beans with pasta and rice. The main reason was Marco was home more — smart working — and he was used to eating pasta at lunch, even at the mess hall, and so we did a family meal at lunch and then again at dinner. I also baked a lot, but this was to make my kids happy. I was now good at making pizza dough as well as focaccia bread. I even made cheesecakes, the Italian version with ricotta cheese, and the American version with cream cheese, as well as banana bread, scones, cookies, brioche, even Italian *taralli*. I know we ate a lot more, clearly emptying out the refrigerator each week. I don't think my kids were ever this well fed, they looked healthy with their plump, colorful cheeks. In less than a month, I had those same cheeks. I also lost the improved tone in my glutes and lower legs and my newfound strength and endurance disappeared.

There were many other coronavirus podcasts but one that I thought would have longevity and not disappear during or after the pandemic was *The Distance: Coronavirus Dispatches* by Vice Audio. Vice is best known for its mix of provocative programming and cutting-edge documentary-style reporting. I appreciated this simple, first-person storytelling podcast. I felt like it was an audio scrapbook, and that I might refer back to it one day to learn about what life was like for random people during the coronavirus. The four-minute stories, or dispatches, were both common and uncommon, relatable and unrelatable.

I found comfort in learning from Don Giovanni Gusmini that the sick were not dying alone in Italy.[107] The 45-year-old priest from Bergamo, one of the Italian cities hit hardest by the pandemic, explained that despite what was being reported there was always

---

[107] Gusmini, Giovanni, narrator. "Last Rites." *The Distance: Coronavirus Dispatches*, Vice Audio, 2 April 2020, play.acast.com/s/dispatchesfromsocialdistancing/lastrites

someone, a doctor, nurse, priest, near the severely ill during their last moments. I found journalist and writer Una Mullaly's nightly ritual of lighting a candle in the window of her Dublin home to be a powerful gesture.[108] The old tradition, something that the Irish would normally do for someone who was sick or had a big exam coming up, caught on during the pandemic. I found courage in the words of Swedish Dr. Cecilia Söderberg-Nauclèr.[109] She said that because of her country's herd immunity strategy, the government wasn't mitigating the spread of the virus and soon the healthcare system would be overwhelmed. She questioned her country's leadership and said it was getting too late and too risky for Stockholm. I found Katie Biniki's plea for help to be moving.[110] The emergency room nurse from Denver, Colorado was in the Middle East to help refugees in camps but when the coronavirus spread, the borders closed. She made her way into Iraq but once she got to the American consulate in Erbil, they weren't sympathetic and denied her request to be sent home. They pointed to the existing travel advice and said she shouldn't have been there in the first place.

Each time I listened to this podcast I thought about what my dispatch would be. I imagined it something like this: I'm Rosamaria, I'm an American expat living in Germany with my Italian husband and two young kids. I'm (curse word) scared. I know Germany has been described as one of the safest countries to be in thanks to its first low coronavirus death rate.[111] I even had a good friend from New York email me and say, "if I could pick anywhere in the world to live during a time like this, it'd be Germany," but I'm still not

---

108. Mullaly, Una, narrator. "Irish Candles." *The Distance: Coronavirus Dispatches*, Vice Audio, 3 April 2020, play.acast.com/s/dispatchesfromsocialdistancing/irishcandles

109. Söderberg-Nauclèr, Cecilia. "Herd Immunity." *The Distance: Coronavirus Dispatches*, Vice Audio, 9 April 2020, play.acast.com/s/dispatchesfromsocialdistancing/herdimmunity

110. Biniki, Katie. "Stranded in Iraq." *The Distance: Coronavirus Dispatches*, Vice Audio, 1 April 2020, play.acast.com/s/dispatchesfromsocialdistancing/strandediniraq

111. Bennhold, Katrin. "A German Exception? Why the Country's Coronavirus Death Rate Is Low." *The New York Times*, 4 April 2020, nytimes.com/2020/04/04/world/europe/germany-coronavirus-death-rate.html

comforted. I worry about what will happen to my kids if my husband and I were God forbid to get sick and need to be hospitalized. It's just us, who would take care of them? Where would they end up? In social services? I can't go back to Italy, it's too dangerous. I would go to New York, where my family lives, but even if we could get there it's too risky without health insurance. I'm trapped.

In the evenings, thankfully, I put all my worries on pause. I didn't think about how overwhelmed I was trying to do my work and help my daughter with hers. I didn't feel so exhausted after a full day of taking care of my kids, keeping up with the household chores, and cooking different meals. I forgot about it all and could breathe easier when I watched my beloved Italian soap opera. Yes, an Italian soap. The show, called *Un posto al sole*, translated to "A place in the sun," was the only thing I regularly watched on television besides the news.

I got into the soap when we first moved to Germany. I should point out that I started watching before we had a Smart TV and Netflix and Amazon Prime had become all the rage. The house didn't have internet when we first arrived, and our TVs mostly picked up national German channels. I quickly got an education from my husband about communication satellites and learned that the problem was that the antenna dish on our roof was pointed to Astra, located at 19.2 degrees, and that's where German television is broadcast. This meant we had a plethora of German channels and only about two familiar channels from *RAI*, the Italian state broadcaster. In order to watch our existing subscription-based package of channels, we had to add an antenna dish to the roof, and it had to point to Hot Bird, 13 degrees. I still don't understand why but it took about two months for this to happen.

The soap, which has been on television since 1996, was one of the only shows I had access to on television during this time. I felt desperate. It was August, summer, when the days were long, and we were newbies trying to get acclimated to our home, our new way of life. I'm not being overly sentimental, but the show set in scenic Naples, my husband's birthplace, in some ways represented a piece of the Italy I had left behind. It also helped me escape a bit and immerse myself in other people's problems, which were much bigger than mine. I quickly grew interested in the characters, Serena, Filippo,

Roberto, Marina, Guido, and Nico, to name a few, and their intertwined lives, and when they finally installed our antenna, and the internet was running I kept watching. The show aired about 30-minute episodes on weekdays at around 8:45 p.m., when I was putting my daughter to sleep. I watched religiously on the TV in her room, but when the coronavirus halted production I was cut off quickly. I was sad, Covid-19 had taken away my show.

So, it was back to the podcasts. Fired up by my soap experience, I wondered whether audio dramas, also known as fiction podcasts, might be escapist enough for me. This was a genre I never considered in the podcast form. I was a journalist junkie. But in the U.S. audio storytelling had recently seen a renaissance[112] (unlike in the UK where audio drama has always been a fixture). In fact, I started with the *BBC*, listening to the world's longest running drama *The Archers,* the daily radio soap (available also as a podcast), which has been around since 1950 and has aired over 20,000 episodes. I jumped in and listened to a few episodes, but I found that it was hard to get into it. I didn't know the characters. Who is Phoebe? Who is Justin Elliot? What about Shula? I was lost and didn't have the energy to put the pieces of this giant drama puzzle together.

Instead, I found *Gossip,* a scripted US comedy from writer Allison Raskin. The show, a Stitcher production that debuted in 2018, focused on three female friends at their weekly coffee meetup. The women, who ranged in age from their early 20s to their 40s, gossiped and talked about the rumors in their small town in New York State called Golden Arches. I immediately wanted to be the fourth person at their small table. I would have ordered my usual coffee drink, a non-fat, decaf mocha, no whip cream, to sip on while we all got caught up. I listened to *Gossip's* 12 episodes in about a week, and since there was no second season, I had to find something else.

I tried the highly regarded fiction podcast called *Limetown* about the mysterious disappearance of some 300 people at a neuroscience research facility in Tennessee. The narrative, told from the

---

112. Dibdin, Emma. "6 Podcasts for the Drama Lover." *The New York Times*, 15 Aug. 2019, nytimes.com/2019/08/15/arts/podcast-dramas.html

perspective of a reporter, was interesting and strong, so strong that it became a live-action TV series for Facebook Watch in 2018, but I didn't like the podcast's resemblance to a non-fiction, true crime podcast. I might as well have turned to one of the true crime, serialized podcasts waiting to be listened to in my library, including *The Shrink Next Door* about a New York therapist who manipulated his patients into taking over their lives, or *Veleno,* an Italian drama about 16 children who were forced away from their families on the outskirts of Modena. I also wasn't getting lost and wrapped in *Limetown,* which is what audio drama should surely do.

I didn't have that problem with *The Diarist.* The show, a neo-noir fiction written by Donna Barrow-Green, told the story of a naïve secretary Andrea Davies who submits to a love affair with her domineering and abusive boss Richard Hayes. Andrea quickly ends up in a maze of deception. I was into the story, set in 1950s New York City, the characters, and the music and the sound effects only helped. I called Richard everything in the book while I listened, including "sicko," "animal," and "liar." I wanted Andrea to be strong, to not do as she was told, and to understand that Richard was manipulating her, but she didn't get it. I wished a friend or family member would have intervened and helped her. I thought a lot about women as I listened, and how vulnerable they, we, can be at times. I was once involved with an older colleague who clearly took advantage of my naivety. I was young, fresh out of college, had just started a full-time job as a reporter, and he was older and more experienced. I was insecure and didn't yet know how to stand my ground. Luckily, I learned quickly, thanks to advice from the strong females in my life, and the experience helped me to grow.

I especially worried about women in Europe battling to stay alive at home with their abusive partners during the coronavirus lockdown. The news media had reported heavily about them, and advocates called on government leaders worldwide to put women's safety first as they responded to the pandemic. In Italy, femicides are increasingly widespread/endemic. Italy has ratified international conventions on curbing violence against women, but the country's complicated legal system has been ineffective when it comes to protecting them. And during 2020, the first year of the Covid-19 lockdown, there were 109 femicides, nine per month.[113] The situation is so run-of-the-mill that since 2007 state broadcaster *RAI* has aired a show called *Amore Criminale*, translated to "Criminal Love." I've watched episodes of the show that told one single "love" story that ended with a homicide. I always wished there would be a better ending, one in which the victim got away and survived, but that was never the case. *The Diarist* didn't end happily either. The protagonist Andrea never got the mental help she needed and remained trapped with her abusive husband. I don't believe there will be a second season, but if that were to happen, we all know how things can change on a whim in dramas. There's always hope with fiction drama.

I liked the genre so much that I looked for other fiction podcasts to listen to at night. I skipped the popular and successful weird horror dramedy *Welcome to Night Vale* about the town's strange events, but that didn't mean I ruled out larger-than-life fiction. I got into *The Amelia Project*. The podcast, by theatre company Imploding Fictions, is about a secret agency that helps desperate individuals to fake their deaths and essentially disappear. The amusing dark comedy was not a serialized story. The 20-minute single episodes were lighthearted and even offered me moments of laughter. The comedy came from the ridiculous situations, such as the scorned wife looking to get back at her cheating husband, the comedian who lost his sense of humor right before the Academy Awards he's scheduled to host, and even Santa Claus who wants out of his gig before X-mas. I found the Italian guys — Joey and Salvatore — who are part of the muscle when it comes to pulling off the so-called deaths to be extremely likable despite their terrible Italian accents. I was grateful that isolation didn't make me want to disappear or start a new life as someone else.

---

113. Di Cristofaro, Chiara and Simona Rossitto. "Femminicidi e violenza aumentano, che cosa stiamo sbagliando?" *Il Sole 24 Ore*, 25 Nov. 2021, ilsole24ore.com/art/femminicidi-e-violenza-aumentano-che-cosa-stiamo-sbagliando-AE4j6LY?refresh_ce=1

Now what?

I never stopped thinking about what would come next. And now it was year three and I was going to say *tschüss* and *auf wiedersehen* to Germany soon. I was leaving the boondocks. I was getting out of here soon. Of course, I wanted to go back to America. I wanted to live in New York, near my family, but I was willing to go anywhere in the United States even if it wasn't in the Eastern Time Zone, at least it would be the same continent. I regrettably, though, wasn't on schedule to finish my PhD by the end of our fourth and final year in GK, and therefore I didn't have a real chance of getting a full-time academic job in the United States, one that offered more to our family. So regrettably, Marco's job still came first and that meant it was back to Italy. Ugh.

The big question was where, what region, in what city or town in Italy. There was no guarantee Marco would return to Rome where he was stationed before his assignment in GK. I had heard worrying stories from the Italian wives about my husband's colleagues who had been sent to remote Air Force bases in Sicily. The secluded destination was a sort of payback for having been one of the lucky few to have an international experience. I already told Marco that there was no way I could live in Sicily. I could vacation on the beautiful island and eat lots of cannoli but to live there full-time would probably destroy me. I could only handle so much. I was back in that state of disarray, the same one I was in when we were deciding about GK, but it seemed worse. I felt tense and my *cervicale*, with headaches and neck pain, was acting up.

I was particularly worried about where my daughter and my son would go to school. I definitely didn't want to send them to public school in Italy. I had read a lot about Italy's underfunded education sector, especially when compared to other European countries. The latest data from UNESCO Institute for Statistics[114] showed that Italy spent 4.1 percent of its GDP on education in 2021. In that same year, Germany spent 4.5 percent of its GDP on education; France, 5.2 percent, and the UK contributed 5.3 percent. The years of government cutbacks were evident from the run-down exterior of the Italian school facilities. There were so many schools in a state of disrepair. They were eyesores. They needed to be renovated. They needed their grass cut and fences fixed and painted. They needed their worn and tattered flags replaced. Every time I walked or drove past one of these schools, I went off on a rant. I just couldn't believe that these were schools that children regularly attended. I couldn't imagine dropping my kids off at one of these places. I'd been inside a few of them to vote during elections, and while the interiors looked a bit better than the exteriors, they were far from engaging and reflected outdated models of teaching/learning — no technology, just desks and chairs facing forward towards the chalkboard, very teacher centric. I wanted my kids to go to a beautiful, inviting school, and my daughter was already doing that by commuting over the border to the international school in the Netherlands. The school offered her a quality education and also considered her status as one of those Third Culture Kids (TCKs), a term coined by US sociologist Ruth Hill Useem[115] in the 1950s for children raised in a culture other than their parents. The school paid attention to cross-cultural communication, multiculturalism, and diversity even at the elementary level.

I thought it would be hard for my daughter (and also for me), who had now spent most of her life here in GK, to attend one of those run-down looking schools in Italy. I imagine that she would miss forest school, where she connected with nature and developed teamwork and problem-solving skills. Or the big sports field with an Olympic-sized track for running and playing. I knew, of course, she would adjust if she had to (not so sure about me), but I promised

---

114. "Government expenditure on education, total (% of GDP) - Italy, France, United Kingdom, Germany." *UNESCO Institute for Statistics*, September 2023.

115. Mayberry, Kate. "Third Culture Kids: Citizens of everywhere and nowhere." *BBC Worklife*, 18 Nov. 2016, bbc.com/worklife/article/20161117-third-culture-kids-citizens-of-everywhere-and-nowhere

myself that if I couldn't send both my kids to an international school, which in Rome would cost about €25,000 euro each per year (I had alrady done some research), they would go to a private Catholic school, which would be at least a few steps up from the Italian public education system.

I began to realize that my daughter and my son were getting the best from our slow-moving life in GK. My daughter liked to collect rocks, sticks, and pinecones, the absolute joy in finding one of those, and digging in the dirt. I now regularly need to use a nail brush to clean her nails. She also enjoyed riding her bike in our quiet village. I didn't have to worry about traffic, just the occasional tractor or harvester. And my son, he was born here, this was all he knew. I felt like he had a little German in him because he hated all Italian cheeses — *ricotta, mozzarella, scamorza*. I didn't know of any Italian or American kid that disliked all of them. And unlike the rest of us, he enjoyed the German sweets, including the *Quarkbällchen* and *Streuselkuchen*. He was also following in his sister's footsteps exploring nature. He had already developed a love for farm animals and tractors and not because he saw them on television but because they were all over our village. I didn't think my kids were sheltered from the "real world" or being raised with an insulating cotton wool-like innocence. They were just living a calm, stress-free life, which is what I started to believe all kids needed.

As we emerged from the pandemic and I began to worry about the future, I found myself changing my views of the place where we were living. Life wasn't so terrible in GK. It was nothing like New York, completely different from Rome, but it was actually pretty good in its own way. I said that, yes I did! I found from my everyday interactions that I — and really, all of us — had better-quality-of-life, especially when compared to Italy. I knew that GK was in the sticks surrounded by acres and acres of farmland. I knew it was simple, somewhat unsophisticated, but for a rural place it was still quite innovative. I started to notice things more when my sister, who studied architecture and works as an educator, pointed out the good, healthy design of the A-frame homes fitted with tilt-and-turn windows (three windows in one — fixed, inswing casement, and hopper), as well as the enthusiastic use of renewable energy and the rainwater catchment systems. And while I always complained about many things and did a lot of comparing and measuring up, I too was feeling more at peace with my calmer, less stressful life.

Unlike in New York or Italy, I no longer used mass transportation regularly. I no longer argued with my neighbor who put a chair in the communal parking to hold his spot. I didn't have to sit through several hours-long, co-op board meetings in which owners argued over what the color of the front door carpet should be. I didn't worry much about security anymore. I didn't live in a complex where there were barred windows and armored doors with five-level mortise locks, which you turned and turned and turned before the door finally opened. I liked living in a place where I didn't have to worry about my car being stolen and where my kids could play safely outside. I was shocked when I first saw what looked like five-and-six-year-old children traveling to and from school by bike or on foot unaccompanied or waiting at the public bus stop alone. I wanted to pick them up and take them home, which would probably be alarming to them and their parents, I know. I would never be okay with my kids doing this, I would have a panic attack, but it did make me feel that we were living in a good place if children could walk home or take public transportation without being kidnapped.

I started to think that if I couldn't go to the United States just yet then it was probably better to stay in GK than return to Italy. I'm not saying that I fit in more here in Germany than I did in Italy. I definitely don't. I adjusted again, tweaked and accepted many things. I made sacrifices so that my kids could have a better, more peaceful, life. I became more mindful of the simple, everyday moments. I also had the GK base where I found pieces of American culture through a number of different stimuli. There was shopping at the base retail store where they sold some comforting American products like Wonder Bread and Pop-Tarts. There were events organized for my kids like the Easter Egg Hunt, Trunk or Treat, and Vacation Bible School. I had Sunday mass in English at the base chapel.

But more importantly, I had all my podcasts and they had evolved so much since their humble beginnings in the early 2000s. I had so much choice and variety. I didn't think of them as one of the best life hacks of recent years because for me they were just so much more. I was a part of the conversation. I listened. I nodded along. I disagreed. I laughed hard. I cried sometimes. I had access to information in a friendly format and that made me feel less scared and insecure. I found that hearing people talk openly about their feelings, thoughts, and experiences, also made me less lonely and cut off from the world. In my ten plus years overseas, it was here in GK that I felt most connected to the United States and to all my interests and it was thanks to podcasts and the hosts of my favorite shows. I was in the know, at least I felt like it, even though I lived in a foreign, somewhat weird, place.

Marco felt the same way about staying. I think he was more convinced than I was. He started looking for NATO civilian staff positions, which offered highly competitive tax-free salaries and lots of other benefits. I knew Marco, if he put something in his head, he worked tirelessly to make it happen. He was all over the NATO civilian staff positions — applying, studying, and preparing for interviews. In our fourth and final year, he was shortlisted for a position as a technician in electronic warfare. This meant he could be called if a vacancy were to open in the next two years, which was good, but was it a job offer, no. I knew he was disappointed, the job was in his area of expertise, unlike the position he was assigned to in GK by the Italian Air Force. I was upset too but at the same time relieved because the decision was made for us. I don't know if that was a sign of weakness, probably so, but I also believed that things went the way they were supposed. I grew up with that mantra.

Six months later things changed. It was mid-December and we had just arrived at Frankfurt Airport and were waiting to check in for our flight to New York. I heard my husband's cell phone ring, but I was busy trying to control my son who insisted on pushing our large luggage even though it was more than double his size. I kept telling him, "No, stop, please, no." I didn't think anything of the phone call, it was just a phone call, but I did notice that Marco was speaking English and so I figured it was work-related. A few minutes later he hung up, looked at me and said, "I got the job. I told them I was still interested. I need to put it in writing after the holidays."

Big news. I was happy for a minute, but then I started to feel nervous about all the unknowns, typical me. I didn't want to think about the NATO job now. I wanted to survive the imminent eight-hour flight with my kids, then relax and enjoy Christmas with my family who I hadn't seen in months. I told my husband that it was better not to talk about the job, and that we would revisit the subject when we returned to Germany. He said okay and we acted as if nothing had happened, as if he hadn't been offered a job that would change our lives again. Even though my husband is not a verbally expressive person when it comes to personal feelings, the fact that he wasn't talking about the job was beginning to weigh on him in New York. He looked worried and had a pale, sickly egg white color about him. I remember that my mother and sister asked me privately if everything was okay with him because they said he didn't look well. I told them that he was offered a NATO job just before our flight but that I asked him not to talk about it during the holidays. They yelled at me and said, "What's wrong with you?"

They were right. They can be brutally honest with me and I don't get offended. They are the only ones allowed to do this. I was being ridiculous, selfish, and so we started to discuss the job offer. The fact that Marco could now talk about it was a somewhat cathartic experience and he even regained some color in his cheeks. We began doing many of the same things we did when we were deciding whether to accept the four-year assignment in GK, including making another pro and con list and pretending we were advising family. We had trouble sleeping, we were restless, but this time it was especially stressful for my husband, because this change not only meant we would stay here for an indefinite amount of time (though, not forever), it would also end his 21-year military career. To accept the position, he had to retire from the Air Force. I think he aged at least 10 years because of this decision, especially since he suddenly had a giant, deep horizontal wrinkle running across his forehead. The other thing was that we were deciding all this during the Covid-19 pandemic when everything seemed scary, up in the air, and unstable. The biggest question was whether it was a good idea to leave his secure, they could never fire him unless he did something illegal and it happened on company time type-of-job.

My family called Marco's decision a "no-brainer," saying that he should take the NATO job, even if it sadly meant that we wouldn't be moving to New York, to the United States. But Marco's own family back in Italy, in particular his mother and eldest brother, strongly advised against it. They called him *"un pazzo,"* a crazy person, for even considering leaving his military job. I knew their advice needed to be taken lightly because it was coming from Italians. The fact is that Italians, including my husband, are not wired to change jobs. Italy is known for its permanently high unemployment rate not its overabundance of opportunities, and therefore if you have a stable, permanent job with a *contratto a tempo indeterminato*, which my husband had, you are told from a young age to hold onto it tightly. It doesn't matter if the job is unsatisfying or badly compensated, you keep it as if it's your safety vest and you're stuck at sea. They even had laws years ago, which have since been abolished, that allowed employees of companies in which the state was the primary stakeholder to give their jobs to their children once they retired. I have a second cousin in Puglia who occupies her mother's former position at the Italian state broadcaster. I've always thought of this as terrible. It must be awful to feel like you can't change jobs because this is the only opportunity you will ever have. Americans change jobs a lot and they do for a number of reasons, such as wanting a new challenge, looking to relocate, escaping a boss, or desiring a bigger paycheck. According to the U.S. Department of Labor's, Bureau of Labor Statistics survey from 2019 the average person in America held about 12 jobs between the ages of 18 to 52.[116] Not Italians.

I wasn't so worried about the weather, the food, the language, the lack of decent clothing and shoe shops, all the things I lamented about over and over again. I couldn't be bitter with Marco for keeping his breadwinner status because it wasn't healthy for our marriage. I had to shift my mindset. I know what I'm capable of and it has to be okay, at least for now. I did feel uneasy about being here for an indefinite amount of time. I tried to sift through and sort this feeling out. I used positive self-talk and told myself that it was good for now but "remember Rosey nothing is forever." I believed that accepting the

---

116. "Number of Jobs, Labor Market Experience, Marital Status, and Health: Results From a National Longitudinal Survey." *Bureau of Labor Statistics, U.S. Department of Labor*, 31 Aug. 2021, bls.gov/news.release/pdf/nlsoy.pdf. Press Release.

position was the best thing, at least for now, and so did Marco. And so, he said yes, he accepted the job, we were staying in GK. Oh my God! Oh my God! I said that a lot for a few weeks. I also realized that by making this decision I wasn't as neurotic as I thought and not so much of an outsider.

I knew that if we were staying, we couldn't keep renting our home, especially because we had already spent thousands of euros during the last four years. I loved our current home and asked the owner if she wanted to sell it to us, but she wasn't interested. I learned that Germans were property owners for life, unlike Americans who buy and sell frequently, because there weren't a lot of homes on the market. Plus, it was hard to actually find or spot the ones that were available. The "for sale" sign was rarely used. I saw that they mostly relied on internet listing services and word-of-mouth. In America they also use online listing services, but this is often coupled with outdoor marketing/advertising, which includes putting up a giant "for sale" sign on the property, usually with the realtor's headshot, along with balloons or some other attention-grabbing thing. This way if someone happened to walk or drive by they would learn about the property's status. The few times I did find a local property online that was interesting, by the time I called I was almost always told it was *verkauft* (sold).

I didn't know what else to do and made an appointment with a local builder to see if he had any houses for sale, and after the meeting I was told that the best thing was to buy a piece of property through the local governments and build our own home. I got us on a few lists of new developments in the GK area and after only about eight weeks we received a reply from the nearby town of Gangelt (remember, where Germany's first Covid case was confirmed). I thought it would take months, which might help me to feel less antsy about home ownership because that meant truly establishing our family here, putting down roots, in Germany, but it didn't. We saw a rendering of the new development and from that we picked one of the plots available, number 159, it was 500 square meters, and based on the map we would have sun (when it shined) in the front of the house in the afternoon, which was what we wanted. I was running in and out of the bathroom kind-of-nervous, but excited.

Then several weeks later we went to the notary's office for the closing where they read and translated word-by-word the entire 20-page document. I found the whole process to be tedious but this was important and so I paid close attention. I heard our translator say something about a five-year limit or cap and I stopped her nervously and asked, "What exactly does that mean?" My brain went into overdrive. Could we not sell the property for five years? What if something better came up? What if we had to get out of here? I was okay with owning land, a home, but I didn't want to feel stuck here for any specific amount of time. If this was a condition I didn't know if I wanted to do this anymore. I looked at my husband with fear in my eyes. I heard the translator ask the notary something and then she explained that we had to complete construction in five years, we could sell whenever we wanted. I took a long, deep breath. I finished listening and then we both signed, we were property owners. The construction began a few months later.

I have a happy home now here, but I still want to get back to New York eventually. I'm not delusional. I'm not acting like a dreamer, at least I don't think so. I know why I have so much love and affection for New York and it's because so many of my memories are there. I grew up happy with my beautiful family. I loved going to college in the city and was enamored with people watching when I rode the 6 train from 23rd street to 68th street each day. I got my first internship at a renowned art gallery in Soho, which not only required me to use my writing skills but also take the gallery owner's Mastiff out for walks. (The dog was bigger than me, imagine that…) I landed my first job in journalism in New York. I worked hard; it felt like there weren't enough hours in the day to write. I was paid so poorly but I learned and grew so much. The city is also where I first fell in love and had my heart broken a few times. I don't know when or how I will get back to New York, but I do know that I definitely don't want to die in Germany. I wouldn't blend in much with the dead either. I look at the obituaries in the local Sunday paper delivered to our home and read the names of the deceased — Jan Schneider, Roger Müller, Anneliese Becker, and Katharina Weber. I couldn't imagine Rosamaria Mancini in there.

If I think about it, I'm probably acting like my father, who first arrived in the United States in 1967, and always compared the United States to Italy, both the good and the bad. He was quite nostalgic about his small fishing town and always said he would return there when it was time to retire. Interestingly though, during our summer vacations he wanted to go back "home" to New York after only about 10 days in Mola di Bari. He found that some of his friends had moved, others had dementia and didn't remember him, and some had even passed away. His childhood home had been completely revamped. His favorite coffee bar now a discount supermarket. I don't know if this will happen to me (I hope not) but if I have learned anything in these now 40 plus years of life, is that I that I need to live for today. I shouldn't think so much about the future but try telling my brain that.

So what's next now that I'm staying here? I'm not waving the white flag. I'm not surrendering myself to Germany and its rule-following lifestyle. I'm still me, a little geeky, bold in my ways, and always ambitious. I have a plan, of course. Here's my lengthy list of what I am going to do:

Continue to listen to podcasts. I had to curtail some of my podcast listening to complete this project, but I need to get back to my favorite shows and I have a long list of new podcasts that I want to listen to badly.

Go back to work full-time. I want to work in communications and also teach at the college level in a more stable role because it's the kind of work that makes me happy. I enjoy being around students (not only because they make me feel young), but because I feel like I can mentor them and help.

Find some stress relief activity, like yoga. I have to stop saying I don't have time. I do this a lot. I have the best gym bag that I can stuff yoga outfits in, aerobic gear, tennis skirts, and all sorts of sneakers but I go once or twice and then stop because something comes up.

Start physical therapy (PT) again. I'm tired of the constant neck pain and headaches. I don't care if I don't understand what the therapists are saying exactly. I mean how much talking is there in PT anyway. I have become pretty good at understanding hand gestures.

Plus, I do know what *sich hinlegen* (lay down) means and can say *Au, das tut weh* (Ow, that hurts!)

Enroll in a legitimate, certificate-yielding German course. I know if I truly learn the language (not just words) then I won't feel like a space cadet and maybe I could fit in more with the locals, especially if I could actually understand and speak to them.

Volunteer so that I connect with people, ones that are physically close to me. I could join the parent teacher organization (PTO) or be a part of the Christmas Fayre committee at my kids school. I think it would be good because technically I will have something to do while I try to socialize.

Visit New York at least twice a year. I know that being surrounded by my family is good for me. I always come back from New York with a healthy glow.

Visit Italy at least twice a year as well. I know that it makes my husband happy to see his family (and me too). Plus, the food and shopping in Italy is hard to beat.

Turn this written account into a podcast. I need to pay homage to the digital media form that's helped me to stay sane and survive in Germany, but also made me feel like I had friends in my corner who understood me so well. I'm thinking of a limited storytelling podcast, which has beginning, middle, and end. I need the structure, but if there are major updates that warrant an extra episode or two then why not. I know that I can be flexible. I also believe sharing all of this in an easily accessible podcast form could help someone else feel less catastrophic, less neurotic, less alone, and more human.

THE END

Acknowledgements

This has been one of the most challenging and rewarding experiences and it wouldn't have been possible without the support of my family. I am especially thankful to my husband Marco, who patiently put up with me during this time demonstrating his generosity and love. I also need to thank my two wonderful, funny children, who often served as my audience when I read aloud chapters even though they looked at me with glazed eyes. I also want to thank my mom and my sister, who have always encouraged me. And where would I be without my faith. I thank God for helping me to stay the course. I am grateful to the Blessed Mother because every time I felt nervous or overwhelmed (which was a lot) I imagined myself protected underneath her soft blue mantle.

In addition, I want to thank my friend Maru Saiz for the cover design, and Cambria Publishing for taking a chance on me. I am sincerely grateful. Thank you. *Grazie, Danke!*

www.rosamariamancini.com

List of podcasts

This is me

Koenig, Sarah, host. *Serial*, Serial Productions, 2014 - , serialpodcast.org

Blumberg, Alex and Lisa Chow, hosts. *StartUp*, Gimlet Media, 2014 - 2020, gimletmedia.com/shows/startup

Where the fox and the hare say goodnight to each other

May B., Sarah, host. *Help Me Be Me*, Cloud 10 and iHeartPodcasts, 2014 -, yaywithme.com/helpmebeme

Furlan, Julia, host. *Life Kit*, NPR, 2018 - , npr.org/podcasts/510338/all-guides

Gebären

Huntpalmer, Bryn, host. *The Birth Hour - A Birth Story Podcast*, The Birth Hour, 2015- , thebirthhour.com/birth-stories/

Merten, Vanessa, host. *Pregnancy Podcast*, 2015 - , pregnancypodcast.com

Points, Dana, host. *Pregnancy Confidential*, Parents, Dotdash Meredith, 2016, parents.com/pregnancy-confidential/

Christmas (and a baptism) in Germany

Steves, Rick, host. *Rick Steves Germany and Austria*, 2005 -, podtail.com/en/podcast/rick-steves-germany-and-austria/

Renner, Rona and Christine Carter, hosts. *Happiness Matters Podcast*, The Greater Good Science Center at the University of Berkeley, 2010- 2013, greatergood.berkeley.edu/podcasts/series/happiness_matters_podcast

Rubin, Gretchen, host. *Happier with Gretchen Rubin*, 2015 - , gretchenrubin.com/podcasts/

Trying to worry less, parent more

Frank, Hillary, host. *The Longest Shortest Time*, Stitcher, 2010-2019, longestshortesttime.com/episodes

Lemieux, Jamilah, Lopez, Lucy, Newcamp, Elizabeth, and Zak Rosen, hosts. *Care and Feeding*, Slate, 2013 - , slate.com/podcasts/mom-and-dad-are-fighting

Lock Kolp, Kay, host. *Practical Intuition with Kay*, 2015 - , directory.libsyn.com/shows/view/id/weturnedoutokay

Lumalan, Jen, host. *Your Parenting Mojo*, 2016 - , yourparentingmojo.com/episodes/

Francis, Meagan and Sarah Powers, hosts. *The Mom Hour*, Life Listened, 2015 - , themomhour.com/episodes/

Palanjian, Amy and Virginia Sole-Smith, hosts. *Comfort Food*, 2018-2020, comfortfoodpodcast.libsyn.com

Good Kids, Lemonada Media, 2019 - 2022, lemonadamedia.com/show/goodkids/

McInerny, Nora, host. *Terrible, Thanks for Asking*, American Public Media, 2016 - , ttfa.org

McKesson, DeRay, host. *Pod Save the People*, Crooked Media, 2017 - , crooked.com/podcast-series/pod-save-the-people/

Baldwin, Hilaria and Daphane Oz, hosts. *Mom Brain*, ART19, 2018 - 2020, art19.com/shows/mom-brain

Skimming in my 40s

Skimm This, theSkimm, 2019 - 2023, theskimm.com/skimm-this

Garfield Bob, and Mike Vuolo, hosts. *Spectacular Vernacular*, Slate, 2012 - , slate.com/podcasts/spectacular-vernacular

Gross, Terry, host. *Fresh Air*, NPR, 2007 - ,

npr.org/podcasts/381444908/fresh-air

Zomorodi, Manoush, host. *Note to Self,* WNYC Studios, 2012 - 2019, wnycstudios.org/podcasts/notetoself

Zakin, Carly, and Danielle Weisberg, hosts. *9 to 5ish with theSkimm,* theSkimm, 2018 - , theskimm.com/9-to-5ish

Catholic Fidem

Fulwiler, Jen, host. *The Jen Fulwiler Show,* 2020 - jenniferfulwiler.com/podcast/

Faris, Paula, host. *Journeys of Faith with Paula Faris,* ABC Audio, 2018 - 2020, abcaudio.com/podcasts/journeys-of-faith/

Hahn, Scott Dr., and Dr. John Bergsma, hosts. *Letters from Home,* St. Paul Center for Biblical Theology, 2012 - , saintpaulcenter.libsyn.com

Meckley, Mary, host. *Daily Meditation Podcast,* 2012 - , sipandom.com/blogs/podcast-posts

Pray As You Go, Jesuit Media Initiatives, 2006 - , pray-as-you-go.org/daily-meditation

The Pope's Voice, Radio Vaticana-Vatican News, 2018 - , vaticannews.va/en/podcast/the-voice-of-the-pope.html

Schmitz, Fr. Mike, host. *The Fr. Mike Schmitz Podcast,* Ascension Press, 2015 - , media.ascensionpress.com/category/ascension-podcasts/frmikepodcast/

Swinarksi, Claire, host. *The Catholic Feminist,* 2017- 2020, thecatholicfeminist.com

That crappy feeling

Strayed, Cheryl and Steve Almond, hosts. *Dear Sugars,* WBUR and The New York Times, 2014 - 2018, wbur.org/podcasts/dearsugar

Reinagel, Monica, host. *Nutrition Diva,* Quick and Dirty Tips, 2008 - , quickanddirtytips.com/nutrition-diva/

Mills, Ella, host. *Wellness with Ella*, 2018 - 2023 , deliciouslyella.com/podcast/

List, listen, cross through. Archive.

Fadel, Leila, Inskeep, Steve, Martin, Rachel, and A Martinez, hosts. *Up First*, NPR, 2017 -, npr.org/podcasts/510318/up-first

Conway, Oliver, Sanderson, Valerie, McDonnell, Claire, Miles, Nick, San Pedro, Emilio, Ritson, Alex, Leonard, Jackie, Gallagher, Charlotte, and Tany Beckett, hosts. *Global News Podcast*, BBC World Service, 2017 - , bbc.co.uk/programmes/p02nq0gn

Barbaro, Michael, host. *The Daily*, the New York Times, 2017- , https://www.nytimes.com/column/the-daily

Renell, Jamie, host. *Covert*, Audioboom Studios, 2018 - 2019, audioboom.com/channel/covert

Jarvis, Rebecca, host. *The Dropout*, ABC Studios, 2019 - 2022, abcaudio.com/podcasts/the-dropout/

Crossman, Steve and Joel Hammer, hosts. *The Hurricane Tapes*, BBC World Service, 2018 - 2019, bbc.co.uk/programmes/w13xttt6/episodes/downloads

St. John, Paige, host. *Man in the Window*, Los Angeles Times and Wondery, 2019, latimes.com/projects/man-in-the-window-podcast/

Eating in

Fucito, Antonio, host. *Lo Scassapizza* (Tanzen vs Pizza) 2018 - 2022, anchor.fm/tanzenvspizza

Adachi, Kendra and Michael Van Patter, hosts. *Pizza Nerds*, 2019, pizzanerds.co/the-show/

Oldani, Davide and Pierluigi Pardo, hosts. *Mangia come Parli*, Radio24, 2017 - 2023, radio24.ilsole24ore.com/programmi/mangia-parli?refresh_ce=1

GialloZafferano: le Ricette, Mondadori Media, 2020,

open.spotify.com/show/3S4vXmfX3OkwxESLUPaNwn

Montera, Mariachiara, host. *Lingua*, Storytel, 2019, storytel.com/it/it/series/36583-Lingua-Mariachiara-Montera

Not blinded by the light

Pellisser, Colleen, and Neil Jacobsen, hosts. *The Good News Podcast*, 2017 -, thegoodnewspodcast.fm

Needed: verb form of LOL

Ryan, Katherine, host. *Katherine Ryan: Telling Everybody Everything*, Kathbum, 2020- , open.spotify.com/show/5nJSygNrpIQRUAMvFhB2YO

Wheelan, Brooks, host. *Entry Level with Brooks Wheelan*, All Things Comedy, 2017 - , allthingscomedy.com/podcast/entry-level

O'Hare, Brendan, and Cory Sneakrowski, narrators. *This is Branchburg*, Abso Lutely Productions, 2019 - 2020, adultswim.com/podcast/this-is-branchburg

Correale, Pete and Sebastian Maniscalco, hosts. *The Pete and Sebastian Show*, iHeartPodcasts, 2016 -2022, iheart.com/podcast/867-pete-and-sebastian-show-30516771/

Netflix is a Daily Joke, Netflix, 2021 - , netflix-is-a-daily-joke.simplecast.com

Productively isolating

McEvers, Kelly, host. *Consider This*, NPR, 2020 - , npr.org/podcasts/510355/considerthis

Robach, Amy, and Aaron Katersky, hosts. *ABC News Radio Specials*, ABC Audio, 2020 - , abcaudio.com/podcasts/radio-specials/

GermanPod101.com, 2008 - , germanpod101.com

Easy German, Easy Languages, 2019 - , easygerman.org/podcast

Coffee Break German, Radio Lingua, 2013 - , coffeebreaklanguages.com/coffeebreakgerman/

Coronavirus Global Update, BBC World Service, 2020 - 2021,

Gupta, Sanjay, host. *Chasing Life*, CNN, 2020 - , edition.cnn.com/audio/podcasts/chasing-life

The Distance: Coronavirus Dispatches, Vice Audio, 2020, vice.com/en/series/krkbn6/podcasts

The Archers, BBC Radio 4, 1950 - , bbc.co.uk/programmes/b006qpgr

Gossip, Allison Raskin and Stitcher, 2018, stitcher.com/show/gossip

Limetown, Two-Up, 2015 - 2018, twoupproductions.com/limetown/podcast

Nocera, Joe, host. *The Shrink Next Door*, Wondery/Bloomberg, 2019, wondery.com/shows/shrink-next-door/

Trinica, Pablo, and Alessia Rafanelli, hosts. *Veleno*, la Repubblica, 2017, repubblica.it/podcast/storie/veleno/stagione1/

The Diarist, Donna Barrow-Green and Illuminus Audio Productions, 2018, illuminusproductions.com/the-diarist/

Baldwin, Cecil, host. *Welcome to Night Vale*, Night Vale Presents, 2012 - , welcometonightvale.com

The Amelia Project, Imploding Fictions, 2017 - , ameliapodcast.com/listen-now